A Word Before I Go
a memoir

BARBARA WHITLEY

Clouds of Magellan Press | Melbourne

© 2020 Barbara Whitley and Garry Kinnane

First published in Australia in 2020
All rights reserved.

ISBN: **978-0-6487469-0-4** – paperback
ISBN: **978-0-6487469-1-1** – ebook

Clouds of Magellan Press, Melbourne
www.cloudsofmagellanpress.net

Distributed by eBook Alchemy
www.ebookalchemy.com.au

Cover images: courtesy of Garry Kinnane
Design: Gordon Thompson

Contents

Introduction by Garry Kinnane ... v

1. Shallows & Shoals ... 1

2. Choppy Water ... 22

3. On the Wrong Track ... 39

4. Backwash of the War ... 52

5. Finding a Direction ... 62

6. Billowing Sails and Blithe Passage ... 74

7. The Course Changes ... 112

8. The Winds Drop ... 121

9 Moving Out of the Doldrums ... 141

10. Come Elements of Youth and Age ... 163

11. L'Envoi ... 189

Introduction

Barbara Whitley (1911-1997) grew up in Balmain, Sydney, the third youngest of ten children. Living in a large family had a shaping influence on Barbara's outlook; she understood well the dynamics of relationships between family, friends, neighbours or lovers, and always sympathised rather than judged, always saw people's humanness rather than their failings or their politics. This is not to suggest she was a saint; there was always a bit of devil in Barbara, something of a rebel, and this also had its beginnings in her childhood, when all the 'responsible' roles seemed to be taken up by her brilliant older brothers and sisters. This roguish side to Barbara comes through her writing of *A Word Before I Go*, especially the early chapters where she deals with her sexual adventures, which she does with surprising frankness for a woman of her generation. But if there could be a single term to describe what drove Barbara, it was *love*; and in return she received it from all who knew her – from her husband(s), her daughter and grandchildren, her wider family and the legions of friends she made everywhere she worked, played and lived. I believe that love, in many forms, comes shining through the elegant prose of this memoir.

Barbara had long harboured a desire to write, but she didn't get around to it until she was in her sixties, when in a burst of creative energy she wrote and published under the pseudonym 'Barbara Foy' a number of short stories in various magazines, one of which 'Up Balmain' was read on ABC Radio. She then under her own name edited her mother's diaries, published as *The Chronicles of Suzy Em* (1977) for which she received a

Literature Board Grant. This was followed by a memoir of her Sydney childhood, called *Kid Sister* (1994). At some point she began what was intended to be an autobiographical novel, which she continued to tinker with over several years, never being able to quite get it ready to offer a publisher. She had given it various titles and had given her first person narrator and some characters several fictional names, in an attempt to produce a novelistic effect. But when I read the typescript, left in her papers after her death, it struck me that this was clearly a memoir that dealt honestly with the real events of her own life. I knew this, as did her daughter (my wife) Jo, from her own extensive knowledge of her mother's life acquired over the years. By this time the main reasons for her writing it as fiction – family sensitivities and her own need to distance herself from the material – had passed, and so I took the decision, with Jo's agreement, to publish it as a memoir, which I believe it truly is. I saw from the start it was too well-written and too interesting to be left moldering in a drawer. It had relevance not just to family and friends but also as a chronicle of its time and settings for any interested reader. So here it is, freshly edited and tidied up, an account of her adult life by an intelligent, independent-minded, talented woman.

Garry Kinnane, March, 2020

1. Shallows and Shoals

I'm not a person who lives in the past, or the future either. I very much believe that right here and right now is the only time there is to be alive. But I'm in my seventies, and I feel I should get myself busy with some clearing out operations so that I don't leave an untidy jumble behind for someone else to go through and dispose of. The physical jumble is nearly impossible; it consists mainly of cloth and paper I can't bear to throw out. It can be done, and is an intermittent process – dear old clothes, precious letters, treasured newspaper clippings, cherished old snaps and photographs – all those things shoved into the cupboard in the hall these years, are slowly being brought to order.

But I find there are some things in the cupboard of my mind that I would like to clear up and leave tidy before I go above or below as the case may be. Just for my own sake. No one can do this job for me, as no one even knows what's there, the unresolved things, unfinished and left hanging. It's the old story, to write them out won't resolve but it should clarify.

Chance has shaken out such a one, right from the back of the cupboard, from the time when I was at school. I suppose most of us can remember, among the indignities of childhood, one of the most painful – being blamed for something you didn't do. I can remember the sad time it happened to me.

LETTER TO KATHLEEN

How long since we last met? Forty years ago anyway. How long since a Christmas card? Twenty or more. In remembering the tremendous friendship we had at school, things tucked away and never thought of are now being recalled as lively, exciting or painful as when we were in our teens. At Sydney Girls High School. I think I was in third year, therefore fourteen, when I came home from school and said to my mother,

'There's a girl at school in fourth year called Kath Foy.'

'Foy,' said mum, 'I wonder. There are only two Foy families in Sydney, Mark Foy's and my father's. The Mark Foys are Catholic. Ask her if she's a Catholic.'

So I approached you, first time of speaking, to ask you if you were a Catholic. No you weren't.

'Oh, ho,' says Mother. 'Go and ask her if her father's name is William.' No it wasn't.

'Let me think,' says Mother, 'ask her if her grandfather's name was William.'

Yes it was. So your grandfather was William, the eldest of old William's first family; and my mother was Emma, seventh child of his second one. Long lost relations we were! In form three, I was junior, and you in form four, a senior. I wouldn't have said Hullo or Boo to you if it hadn't been for this. But once introduced and by so intriguing a bond, we found affinity between us, with lots to say. Soon, though, we became aware that not only was it judged unseemly for a junior and a senior to be friends, it was just about illegal. We could feel the weight of an unwritten law heavy on our friendship. So we didn't lunch together or be together in playgrounds, we just smiled a heart-to-heart smile when we happened to cross paths. We had to make up for it as best we could out of school, and living in suburbs well apart. But Oh, how close we were! It was my first friendship with a girl, I who grew up among brothers. I had a girl to talk with, just at the time when I needed one – I was like a little crucible simmering on the hob, full of strange new ingredients that I didn't know what to do with, didn't even know what they were. Little innocent, I knew nothing about life or sex or the world outside my home and school. I was all one lump of awareness of beauty in the natural world, sunsets, moonlight, our great garden with the magic of its trees in all of their moods – the big Morton Bay fig-tree teeming with chattering sparrows morning and evening – the changing patterns and colours of the Harbour and the delights of the little ferry journey across to town. The days of playing with my brothers were just about over, my big sisters were in worlds of their own; in a family of ten I had been lonely. And now I had a friend. I was transported with bliss. My feet were off the ground; but only till they were brought back where they belonged with a very nasty thud. It was made known to me, not directly but very painfully, that this wonderful friendship was a wrongdoing at my door; I shouldn't be friends with you because (for Heaven's sake) you were a senior. It was the first disenchantment of my life, and a bitter sad one.

So we were together whenever we could manage it. We talked and talked, long, long talks. In absence we wrote and wrote, long, long letters. And often took to poetry, so-called. In a way I could weep now to think of this being the only spill-over for that little crucible – so much to be learnt about and known and I spent my spare time writing verses about trees in the moonlight! No wonder that when I went to university and was swooped upon by the intellectual Julian for my pretty face and was found to be a mental baby, he told me that I was like a piece of round pink bath soap trembling on the edge of the bath.

To go back to the pen-on-paper, I wasn't the only one. It was the fashion to have a crush on Kath Foy (there was no law against a common-or-garden crush), and clearly I can see you in your brown uniform with your top blazer pocket bulging with letters. Do tell me, how did you do all your homework and collect those stunning honours in the Leaving, with all those letters to read and write? Somehow you did.

In this way our friendship burgeoned till, trying for a special scholarship, you repeated fifth year; we were as if by magic then peers because in the same year, and for English, Latin and Greek if I remember, in the same class. Ancient history as well. I wasn't up with you in Maths and French. In a way I could weep again, looking at that list of subjects and thinking of the sheer slog of study that went into them (through university as well), and of the more useful things I could have spent my labour on! Pleasure, enjoyment, delight – but useful for battling the big world? Not that I had a vestige of a notion then that I would be doing any battling and needing useful qualifications.

My little drama must have begun when I was in fourth year, and you not only in fifth but School Captain as well. Though I was now an official senior, it seemed that our friendship was still in disfavour. I could still feel myself being frowned on and disapproved of, not by the girls I think, but the teachers I was sure thought me a sinner. Not that I had been saint in just ordinary school ways, as we remember! I have a dim memory of our Principal once calling me the naughtiest girl in the school, but that was entirely different, and if anything a prideful eminence. Just plain being naughty was a game on my part; if a teacher was giving me a good lesson I was perfectly docile and receptive; if she wasn't I thought it up to me to enliven the period and make it entertaining somehow. No, it wasn't that (and anyway one stops being naughty by fifteen). There was something else they had against me, and my innocence thought it was my tenacious friendship with you. That they weren't frowning on you was something this same innocence didn't think of.

I still wonder what it was, what it even could have been. I realised later that it must have been something pretty awful that someone was up to, someone mistaken for me perhaps? Something to do with –hush – boys? It was beyond the pale, anyway. When the school excursion was for Kosciusko and my name was on the list to go, I believe the teacher in charge fearfully exclaimed, 'Not Barbara Hall!' And Oh the grief, the hurt, the misery, when Mavis, Jean, Meg, Sheila and Co., the immediate friends of fourth year, were all elected prefects, but not Barbara Hall. A pain alleviated at the time when I heard that the school vote had me well up on the list but the staff wiped me off. But why? What had I done? What was my sin?

Dear Miss Brewster sent for me, Deputy Principal and Science Mistress. She had always taken an interest in Hall girls, as well she might, two of them having been her star pupils and burnishing her with a Top of the State in Botany two years running. They were at university by the time I started High School, and I was a sad disappointment to her. I was far from the model pupil she was expecting me to be, and also I chucked Botany at the end of first year and chose to do Greek. A fine lady, firm, honest, and dedicated, Miss Brewster, who had us all in the holy terror of awesome respect.

'Barbara,' she said sorrowfully to me, 'do you know what they are saying about you?' (Bless her, she didn't believe it, whatever it was). But Oh for my innocence! Oh for the forthright old William Foy! I hung my head in shame and whispered, 'Yes, Miss Brewster.'

Self-confessed I stood, and to this very day I don't know to what. And never will. But more than fifty years on, I wish I could tell Miss Brewster it wasn't me ...

*

I was just seventeen when I left school, and even for 1929 I think now, unconscionably innocent. At least I did know in theory where babies came from, and there had been a Normie or two who used to take me to the pictures and give me boyish kisses at the front gate afterwards, in the shadow of the old Morton Bay fig tree. All my last two years at high school I used to wish I had a boyfriend, and the status thereof. I yearned to belong to the dashing small coterie of girls who had real partners bringing them to school dances (as distinct from brothers) and who were lambent with an air of 'I know something you don't know.' They would shut up if I came upon them talking, and Oh the indignity of hearing them say, 'We couldn't tell you'! Innocence, thy name was certainly Barbara in those days.

I didn't even know I was pretty. From the merciless teasing of my two older brothers, I believed myself the fattest and ugliest girl in Australia. History relates that I was indeed puppy-plump, but ugly I was not, and of course I was shining with the glow that Nature puts about her seventeen-year-old nubiles.

LETTER TO JULIAN

To the University with my trails of innocence I went. You beheld me. And fell, head over turkey.

I wonder if you are still alive? And I wonder if you ever forgave me, not just with the passage of time, but with real understanding? The progress of your own life, in the 50 years since those far-off university days, would have rolled away the pain I caused you, but was it ever forgiven? I can only forgive myself because of the poor excuse – I couldn't help it.

You came up to me in the quad one day, tall thin fellow with very shiny goldy hair and an intense sort of face, and asked me if I would go to the ballet with you. To see Pavlova! I was all mixed up in thrills; had never seen ballet before, for a start, and to see the fabulous Pavlova was beyond all dreaming. Such a splendid invitation, and it's coming from a young man! Could this mean that I was on the verge of having a boyfriend, at last?

Permission was obtained from parents, after you were brought home to be inspected; half-way given because my mother knew your mother at church. We went to the ballet, in the best seats, you in a dinner suit, I in my only evening dress, green lace with dippy bits at the sides, and I had a loan of my sister's beautiful yellow silk shawl with its long golden fringe.

A memory of sheer magic and enchantment, that evening. Did you begin to find me out then, and that behind that blooming face was a baby mind that knew nothing of music, art, life, love? Of literature – English – I did know a smidgen, but nothing later than the Romantic Revival, as 'done' in school. Anyhow, find me out you soon did, and joyfully set yourself the job of educating me.

You received an allowance from your mother once a month, and then you would have a splash, all on me. You began in bookshops. I would come out of a lecture and you'd be in the quad waiting with a book for me, no library book but bought, new. Bernard Shaw you idolised, so you started me off on *Plays Pleasant*, which was fine, but I wasn't so sure about *Plays Unpleasant*. Ibsen was there too – had I even heard of Ibsen? Galsworthy, Trollope, Samuel Butler, Stevenson's *Vailma Letters*, Georgian poetry (also a little shocking). I can't remember them all, but you would find a spare sprinkling in my bookshelves yet, with *Barbara Hall, 1929*, written by you inside the cover. Music wasn't so easy, you had to start from scratch there, but you took me to all the concerts you could afford, and I did my best to enjoy them without getting sleepy – in piano recitals I managed best. I suppose you hoped that some knowledge was getting rubbed into me.

I lapped all these interesting things up with gusto, and thought you were wonderful, though you didn't quite fit the pattern I thought a boyfriend should. You took me to university balls, indeed, which was more like it, but I thought you couldn't dance, and you thought I couldn't. So then you invested in very exclusive, private classes just for the two of us, from Sydney's best ballroom dancing teacher – was his name Carl Thomas? I can still hear the music from *Showboat*, the very latest musical, played on a wind-up gramophone while the poor fellow did his useless best to make us dance well together. One of the first dances we went to was at the Women's College. When you took me out into the garden and found a seat in a sheltered nook, I thought, 'Ah it must be coming at last, the real boyfriend business'. But all you did was make charming speeches to my beauty, in elegant prose, until the whole dance was over and then made to take me back. Bold baggage Barbara, what did she say in her astonishment? 'Aren't you going to kiss me?' Poor serious swain, terrified of just that very thing.

I suppose now we were both in the same boat, and you were enchanted with the idea of having a girlfriend. But we had different notions on the matter. Mine were just ordinary, common or garden stuff, but yours were imbued and dripping with high flying romantic ideals – your knowledge of literature was more than just a smidgen. You even wrote poetry to me. No other girl I ever heard of had a fellow who did that. Sometimes in the book you had for me there would be a sheet of foolscap covered with verse, sometimes as I sat working in the library such a sheet would be slipped onto my papers. There was lots of it, and I'm sure it was good too. You always loved words and took pleasure and pains in your use of them. I can remember some of those poems now, truly I can. I even had a go at writing some myself, but those I can't remember, and better not. You did seem to be a very unusual kind of boyfriend, but very exciting. Never a dull moment!

So we went on through the university year, and certainly some kissing came to pass, innocent enough stuff as I recall. You knew much more of me than I of you, though there wasn't much of me to know. I didn't really try to find out what made you tick, I was still a child and concerned with your impact on me. Forgive me!

You told me your story, your father who had been a professor of geology, your mother a rabid Christian Scientist, you the only child – your father who lost his mind and became childish, your mother who tried to cure him by her faith. After his death she had gone to Boston for her recovery from a breakdown. She had just come back when I met you, and was a Christian Science practitioner with an office in the city. You refused to live with her, and were boarding with an old family friend. How you hated the very words Christian Science, how you used to say you hated your mother. You blamed her and her religion for your father's defeat. It was all strange to me, undreamt of, anything but the bland surface of life's design, Mother, Father, Family, and all growing up and everyone loving everyone else, with a rumpus now and then to keep things lively. I was ill-equipped to understand how your experience had affected the highly sensitive, intelligent person you were. I barely had the equipment for the sort of hard thinking I now had to do about my own faith in Christian Science, which was the only religion I myself had ever known till that time. I was bursting open at a great rate, and you so often bewildered me, always trying to talk and sort things through, to comprehend the real truth lying in matters I had always taken for granted. I can remember saying to you once – we were on a ferry on a sweet summer's day – 'Don't you ever stop thinking, and just be?' You gave this strange idea some thought, and then replied solemnly 'No, I don't think I ever do.'

So of course our romance was doomed. I'm trying now to remember how it faded away in my second year, though not entirely. You had your degree and were doing teacher training, and I was having a gay old time. There was a fellow called Jack, a 'divine dancer' who took me to balls, some other fellows and lots of fun, but nothing was serious. Until, at the end of the year when my dad had to go to live in the Blue Mountains because he had tuberculosis, you introduced me to your friend Clarrie, whose family lived there too. Clarrie, also at the University doing Law. And with Clarrie the kissing became something less than innocent, Oh indeed.

What a sorry affair it was. He set out to seduce me right off because, he said, he'd had one girlfriend-ship with no sex in it (not that we ever used that word!), and he wasn't going to have another. He was 22, and he must have made up his mind that he wasn't going to die wondering (boys as well as girls could be virgins at 22 in those days). And I? This was another something I knew nothing about. No word of warning had ever been dropped in my ear, or of wickedness either; no word at all, in my home or Sunday school, of the traps and pitfalls that could beset me, let alone the feelings. And so, blithe as a bonny blackbird and as reckless, I was undone. I did know just enough not to go gaily chatting to my mother about it.

Clarrie wasn't the pattern of a boyfriend either. There was no talk of love, no junketing to the ballet or the pictures even, no going for a surf and coming home together for Sunday tea. There was no kudos in it, no showing off to friends or family. By now I was living in the Women's College, and all I'd have would be a call on the phone any old evening, and we'd go wherever we went, which was no place except in the open air, parks and such and it was a sad enough sort of doings anyway. Precautions were entirely a matter of *coitus interruptus*, and what with youth, ardour, inexperience and the problem of pants and panties, the *interruptus* part would come before very much *coitus*, or even any at all.

However, you were in a job now, teaching in a city school, and we still wrote letters and met now and then. And, still blithe, what did I do? Forgive me forever. I told you. I still don't know why. Did I feel that you were part of my life, and what happened to me must be interesting to you? I had no vestige of a notion what the telling would do to the feelings of your passionate heart, with which you still loved me. What did I know then of the torment of sexual jealousy? Of real passion and desire? You can probably still remember what a cataclysm it was, and perhaps you can remember something which I can't. Why was it that the next thing I knew, I was engaged to be married, to you? I know that, in awful confusion between my feelings for the man who loved me and wanted me for wife, and for the one who only wanted you-know-what, I had had a soul-searching talk with one of my big sisters, and told her all about it. Her advice was, to marry you. Again why? Was she afraid that I was on the road to becoming a 'fallen woman', and thought better I be 'safely married'?

So Clarrie was hove off to the horizon, you gave me a beautiful ring, with a rich purple amethyst set in hand-wrought silver, and we had a brief engagement of three months or so – my last term at university. I wanted to love you, because of the person you were and because of your love for me, but what hope did I have, when another fellow had let the genie out of the bottle, and in spite of myself I wanted that one to love me. And when, now I had that ring on my finger, I had to measure up as a future wife and be perfect, without blemish at all? You would say to me, 'When we're married I hope you still won't go on doing …' whatever it was that bothered you, even wearing a beret. Poor man, you were teaching and boarding, and hadn't had a home life anyway since ages gone; and now, with one in the offing, you were looking for some wifely traits and behaviour. You brought me collars and cuffs to turn and mend – and will I ever forget the time you asked me to make some doll's clothes for the little girl where you were boarding, giving me the size by drawing the doll's outline in chalk on your green note folder?

I couldn't handle all that. I couldn't handle any part of the combination of powerful forces that were tumbling me about. As well as being your fiancée, I was trying to catch up and fag for my finals, and my beloved dad was dying – my first knowledge of grief. At weekends I would be away to the mountains to be with him. When the phone rang at College and the call went up 'Barbara Ha..a..a..ll', my heart would jump, no longer in the hope of hearing Clarrie's voice, but in fear of hearing my dad was dead. No wonder I was as silly as a rabbit, and that our engagement was anything but a happy time. It ended about the same time as the finals; and my dad's life ended then too.

The conclusion of this part of my story doesn't involve you, except for one thing. After those finalities I went away to a holiday job at the beach for a month. Being at Woodford in the vacation had brought Clarrie and me together again, and, knowing I wasn't engaged any more, he made a sort of pact that he would phone me at the end of the four weeks. Which he did. His astonishing news was that in this time he had examined his heart and found he really loved me … and therefore we weren't going to 'do it' any more. If he ever writes any resolvings of old things I wish he would tell me his process of arriving at that fantastic decision. Was he so old school that he believed a man could sow his wild oats where he may, but when it came to love and the woman he might marry, that sort of stuff was 'not done'? Anyhow, a really tortuous time set in. I had the boyfriend act all right, and the usual going to places together, but what I really wanted was access to a good double bed, and I had to have a trip up the aisle to get that. The prospect was in the remote time when Clarrie would be 'through' and somehow, despite the Depression, earning a living. 'Through' as I was myself, I didn't look for a job – couldn't think of anything I wanted to do, except be wed.

For a while you and I kept in touch through letters. I must have still felt you were part of my life, for I wrote and told you how I was aching to be married. How could I have been so unaware of what I had done to you, how could I? In the finish you did what you should have done long since, dipped your pen in fury and gave me a verbal hiding. Which shook me up, put me into a hot blush of desperate shame, woke me up, and at last, shut me up. And you were free for the business of getting me out of your system and finding someone for partner who suited you better than I ever could have done. This you did, and I was invited to your wedding, Oh – five years later? And more than five years later still, we met by chance on the beach at Nielsen Park. Three children, I think, were with you and with me, one. You invited me home to tea. I can remember your wife, though not her name. She made me welcome. When I was leaving your Darlinghurst flat, you skimmed over the bookshelves that lined the whole, picked out and gave me three books. Perhaps I was already forgiven?

*

My mother was forty when I, eighth child and fifth daughter, was born, and the aftermath of World War One was making its terrific impact on the world in my school days; so there was a tremendous generation gap for a start. She thought I would become another pearl just like the other four on her string (seven to eleven years older than I), given the same treatment and handling, and maybe I was a ruby or an emerald, but the same kind of jewel I just was not. Then of course who brought me up? A rather remote father who doted on me, and Nan, eldest sister and second mother to us all, but especially to me. So my mother wasn't very real to me as a person, nor I to her. She was happy enough when I came home with Julian for boyfriend, she always liked him and the directness of his honesty especially — and what's more, she knew his mother. But when I was going through the pangs and pains of eighteen and nineteen she was away in the Blue Mountains looking after Dad; when she came back to Sydney after he died, and set about gathering up her scattered family, she thought she could take me up where she had put me down two years before, and it couldn't be done. There I was thinking I could carry on answerable only to myself as I'd been doing, and not a dutiful daughter or family member at all. Her shocked face one day, how it showed her utter confoundment, when I came to her dressed to go out, to say goodbye, and I hadn't asked her if I could go; and she'd planned for me to help her mend the sheets or whatever that day (not telling me, of course). A little incident, but it showed us both how things stood, and that we'd need to take some care.

Worse than that, where was Julian? Instead of him, this almost stranger, this boy Clarrie, was clearly my inamorato. In fact she could see we were madly in love, and I daresay my sins (bygone though they were) were writ large all over me.

LETTER TO MY MOTHER

We finished up good and loving friends, I delighting in all your rich qualities, and you I think enjoying me. But Oh dear, in 1932 we were way on the other side of that. Strange to think, we never spoke of that time in later years, not one word, and I recall it now probably for that reason. We never resolved it, and it was a desperately miserable time.

My poor mother. You didn't have the equipment for handling an errant daughter. Never had one before. Never expected to have one. You and Dad were always on the watch out for your sons, ever afraid of their straying down the primrose path – it was understandable and regrettable, but not-to-be-surprised-at in a male. Your daughters, not so. In spite of your ten children, I don't think you ever got much joy and satisfaction from sex. Ladies of your era didn't expect to, and the gentlemen didn't expect them to either. It was a rather nasty activity that everyone knew men were addicted to, and when you ladies were married you knew you had to suffer it, but you got your real life satisfaction when you 'held your little child in your arms' (your very own words to a lass about to be wed). A girl like I was, choosing to engage in this pastime – she was not nice at all. If she was seduced against her will, OK that was not her fault and a tragedy that you knew had been around for ever. But to be a free-choice partner? She was beyond the pale, belonged in that shady other world you only vaguely knew existed.

I think you must have been helpless with fear, stripped down to bare maternal instinct, and could do no more than try to keep me in the nest, tucked as safely as might be under what to you were guardian wings, but to me were monstrous thumbs. I was through University, and the next step in the pattern would have been to look for a job. You told me you had always had an ambition to have a 'daughter at home', and with the other four well and truly out in the world I was certainly your last hope. You gave me ten shillings a week pocket money, one afternoon a week off, and I did the cooking for the family, seven of us. I had to ask permission when I wanted to go anywhere at all, bring a fellow home to meet you before I could accept the merest casual invitation, be home by eleven p.m. (or 1 a.m. if I went to a dance), tell you exactly what I was doing whenever I was out of your sight; toe, toe, toe the lines.

You still weren't stark raving certain until you had it in words out of my mouth. The climax came after the day I went up to have my degree conferred. I had woken up sick to my stomach. Cooked lamb's fry for the family breakfast (couldn't face that dish for years afterwards). Got to the University somehow. Cried all through the ceremony, except for my little toddle up to the Chancellor, thinking of my dad and how proud he would have been, just sat there like a fool with tears falling down my face. Home. Straight to bed. Had to cancel the party I'd been going to. And there I lay, poor sick silly little girl. Now was your chance! I was at your mercy. You'd come in with the orange juice or junket, sit yourself down and talk at me, probing, poking, digging and delving for a confession. I would quiver with dread when you came in, a midget before a great ogre. You always did have a fine flair for the dramatic in any situation, and you surpassed yourself in this one. 'If a girl loses her virtue she loses the most precious thing she has … the man will have his pleasure of her and then throw her in the gutter like a squeezed out lemon … no other man will ever want to marry her …' On and on, day after day. Oh Mother, why didn't you just ask me?

There was another big sister staying with us, the married one. In my desperation I confessed to her, and asked her advice. Of course she said I should tell you. So the next time you came in with the lemon barley water, I sat up and confronted you, and in fury. 'What you are thinking about me is right,' says I, 'and it's wonderful and beautiful, and if you make it ugly for me I'll hate you for the rest of my life!' So flopping down and turning my poor brave face to the wall.

I'm still glad I said that. Not that you could do anything about it. For you, ugly it was and a catastrophe of the first size. The only comfort you had was that we'd given up our wicked ways and weren't 'doing it' any more. (It has only just now occurred to me that one reason for your comfort must have been that I wouldn't be getting pregnant.) I don't know what you said to poor Clarrie, when his turn came, which of course it did; he was too paralysed with embarrassment to tell me any of it.

So then we had to live along, and it wasn't much fun for anyone. My poor Mother! What a turmoil of a time in your life! I wasn't the only one whose ways had changed in those two years and who was setting your motherly wings flapping wildly; also you were learning to live without a husband, both emotionally and in business responsibilities. I was a sad case. Clarrie never once broke the vow he'd made to himself, whatever the unintentional temptations put on by a lass who had no conviction about it herself. I was crazy with frustration, and so, I suppose now, was he. Towards the end of the year another sister came to the rescue, bless her. (I don't know how the knowledge of Barbara's fall from grace filtered through the family grapevine, but it did, and of course I didn't realise then that my older siblings had any concern about my affairs.) Mary was Secretary in the Teachers' College at Armidale, and when she heard of a job going as governess on a sheep station near there, she must have thought, 'That's just what my young sister needs, to get the hell out', or was her sympathy for you and your needing me out and off your nerves? She suggested it, I grabbed at it, and away I went.

MRS C. AND MARJIE

How I did enjoy that time! I was a city lass all my life, except for one short holiday on a dairy farm when I was twelve, but I think there must have been a country streak in my genes somewhere. I loved being there. It was a happy time. I was accepted straight away, made part of the family. It was fun with the kids, two boys twelve and nine and young Marjie in between them. The funny little girl; she wouldn't be touched, not by anyone, father and mother included. 'I hate kissing,' she'd say. 'What about Whisky?' I'd ask – he was her little black and white pony, dearly loved, and she'd fondle him all right, and kiss him on the nose. 'Horses aren't people,' she'd answer, with a world of scorn. She hated school too. Lessons out on the verandah weren't too bad, she could look out and away over the wide rolling hills, or nearer to the home paddock, where sometimes Whisky would amble into sight. Then, in the middle of my trying to teach her a thing, she'd let fly with her joyful call – 'Oh-Whisky-Oh!' We could get a bit cranky with each other by the end of the day, but the very second that my watch hands got to 3.30 … 'Come for a ride Miss Hall?' School was one thing, real life another. There was a brown pony, Judy, set aside for me, and a devil she was for not letting herself be caught. We had to trick her, Marjie walking quietly up with the bridle in one hand, hidden behind her back, and an apple in the other, with me in the offing to grab Judy round the neck as she stretched out for the apple. We had some great fun – not that I could ride, but Marjie enjoyed the turn-about of having something she could teach me. A dear child and very loving under her prickles. We finished up good friends.

It was fun learning about station life – a holiday was always declared, and I included, when shearing, crutching, drenching and all were on, even one lovely time mustering. Also the country was beautiful, the wide burnt-gold paddocks, the willows dipping into the creek, the slim up-reaching poplars turning golden in the autumn, and the brilliant evening sky.

But Mrs C., what a lonely lady! Her good sheep-farming husband was no bloke for reading or listening to music, the two solaces and pleasures of her rather isolated life. She'd get a box of books up once a month from a Sydney library, and how she did enjoy having someone to share them with – our tastes were much the same. But I had the bigger win when it came to music. She had a fine collection of classical records, and listening with her was my first real introduction to one of the abiding joys of my life. I'd been to concerts with Julian sure enough, but now I could hear a symphony, concerto, sonata, over and over and get to know it. And love it for ever. Thank you, Mrs C., thank you, thank you.

2. Choppy Water

I came back from the country within a year, much more like myself than before I went. But crunch! Back to the same old silly situation with its frets and frustrations, which really couldn't be borne any longer. Clarrie made the break one afternoon. We were sitting in the Quality Inn in King Street, drinking cup after cup of coffee (first cup sixpence, fill-ups for free), while he told me he thought it would be better if we parted 'for three months' and why? – at least, I don't think he told me the real why, which must have been that he was fed up with me, my mum, and the whole box and dice, and wanted out and away. Of course the three months bit was just to soften the blow, and so came the end of that affair, and my poor little heart was broken.

Now was the time when my mum should have given me a jolly good (metaphorical) kick in what she would have called the BTM, told me to come off it, stop the tragedy queen act, find myself a job and start operating. Not that finding jobs was easy to do in 1933 and the country battling with the Depression. But I could have a go. I find it hard to understand now why I didn't, but just let myself go along, still under those heavy-feathered thumbs, pressed down by her fear. I was still doing the family cooking with ten shillings a week pocket money, taking the little trips to town on Thursday afternoons, and spending a big part of my time crying. I was also spending a small part of the ten bob on cigarettes, which were my friend and consolation as well as means of defying my mother – behind her back of course. I had a secret smoking place out in the garden, and at night I used to creep into a little upstairs attic for a sinful fag – thinking that if she didn't see me, that was enough; which I now suppose it was.

I haven't realised until now, looking back, that my older siblings would have been deeply concerned about me. I thought my troubles were all my own, although I had always been rather a pet 'kid sister'. I took their love for granted, however, and it's interesting too that now was the fourth time that I turned to one of them for help. This time it was brother Pev, a solicitor, eldest of us all, who had a very tender love for me, and must have been very aware of the shocking waste that was going on. He came up with the notion that I should study shorthand and typing. I didn't think much of that, but I had to do something, anything. He wanted me to go to the best school in the city, but at first we could only get mum to compromise on a little local place. I used to trot off there in the mornings, and still be free to be the family cook. But it was the breakthrough, at last, the had-to-come breakthrough. Later I did go to the city school, doing both day and evening classes, until I was good and competent. And then the school found me a job. (And I suppose my mother found a cook!).

A business college isn't (at least, wasn't) any place for forlorn girls to meet fellers, and I didn't. I've forgotten how Ronnie came along. He had daughters older than I was, so he told me, and a wife he didn't tell me anything about (and vice versa, no doubt!).

TO A MIDDLE-AGED ROUÉ

You fancied yourself as a Great Lover, I do believe, and thought to amuse yourself by making a conquest of this ingenuous damsel, this delicious mixture of comely and silly, who had stumbled into your path, and who was clearly lonely for some masculine attention. It was while I was learning shorthand and typing, and Step Number One was getting me into your one-man office to type letters for you (which you had to retype yourself afterwards). Then you take me out to lunch, in a hotel or exclusive restaurant. How flattered I was! What could a sophisticated man of the world see in little me? I had terrible trouble with my clothes, trying to turn myself out to match. I used to make them myself, on the cheap, even my hats, and must have looked a proper frump (as if you cared!). You taught me the niceties of eating out, how to handle grilled flounder, to take lemon in black coffee, to drink champagne, how to hold the liqueur brandy glass in my hands to warm it. A wool buyer, you talked cunningly to my enraptured ears about your travels, about Paris, Rome, New York, London; the ballet and theatre to be seen, the shops and salons with dream-stuff clothes, the famous restaurants with exotic food and wine. I was beside myself with all the glamour you put on.

    I don't know what dodges I used, but Mother didn't know anything about my excursions with you, even when you got to Step Number Two, which was taking me for afternoon drives to secluded little spots around about the foreshores of the Harbour. Only then did I begin to wake up to what you were at. So we got to the kissing. The first time – I remember it yet. Your mouth was soft, moist and a bit slobbery – not the kind of mouth I knew about. At all. And then you leaned back and looked at me, in mock rapture, and said (likewise), 'But that's a miracle!' Something clicked in me; I couldn't have been so silly as not to recognise that for and act. But I let it pass. You were the only male creature taking any interest in me just then, and the only avenue for keeping our wicked secret from my mum. The stops in the secluded places became kiss and cuddle sessions, and you thought you were working nicely along to the great seduction scene, when you made your first mistake. You started telling me about your conquests, the lovely ladies on board ship, or in Paris, Rome, etc, and you kept on in some detail about them, gaily enough – whether they liked your moustache or not, for instance. But instead of inclining me to join the happy throng, you set me feeling uncomfortably certain that I wouldn't measure up.

Step Three was the little picnic hamper in the car, with the cold luncheon of chicken and salads, and of course, champagne. You were closing in, but you settled your own hash and never knew it. A middle-aged gent – in the broad light of afternoon – in the back of a car – sad enough; but my shabby scraps of underwear revealed – too much! On our next occasion, silly man, you chose as your subject for the day those divine little lingerie shops in Florence, with their delicate wisps of crêpe-de-chine undies all adorned with exquisite hand-embroidery and lace. That was the end of that!

FIRST JOB

At last, I had a job. It wasn't much of a one, but it was a tremendous eye-opener. I was in the office of big city hospital, two pounds a week, not doing shorthand and typing, but set to putting a new filing system into operation. Brother Sep said I was lucky to get anything, a senior at 23 and with no experience, so I had to swallow what I had of pride. We were all together in one big room, accountants, stenographers, clerks, and I was in a world I hadn't known existed. They looked askance at this girl with a university degree; one of them told me later they had decided I must have taken the job because I was writing a book, so foreign were we to one another. It was the first time I found that it is useful to keep one's ears open and mouth shut, at least about anything going on around one. I was cheerful enough company, and soon we were all friendly. On Monday mornings they'd manage a quick bit of talk about the doings. The first news was always about their luck, betting on the races on Saturday afternoons; mostly in two bobs on the SP, I imagine their only excitement in a drab enough existence (it was a real breakthrough for me, and rather sinful, the first time I put two bob into a Melbourne Cup sweep). Next would come what they'd seen at 'the pictures' on Saturday night, and their taste was my poison, and vice versa. Then mostly someone would have a smutty joke to tell. There was a certain level beyond which the men wouldn't go in mixed company, but the girls told a few beauties among themselves. My ignorance would laugh brightly, and have to get a brother to put me wise when I got home. Some of the men used to go to the 'footy' on Saturday afternoon, have a pie to eat in town, and then go to the wrestling at Leichardt Stadium at night. By this time I was all for experiencing anything that was going, and was flattered to be so accepted when I was asked along. Perhaps they thought I was putting it into my 'book', but I was just gathering education whenever it came my way, and learning fast.

Our boss was the Hospital Superintendent, and a horrible snob. Doctors, himself included, were gods, just down amongst us from Olympus, noblesse-obliging. Office staff were underlings of inferior race, less than the dust. We were all paid below the then standards – satisfaction of working for the Noble Profession, we were told, should be part of our reward. We wondered how poorly he and those other gods were paid. The job I was employed to do was impossible in the first place, and bend my brains and my fingers as I might, there were way-back muddles and confusions for which he made me feel guilty. He gave me a 'tremble-before-the-boss' complex that was a long time working out of my system. I stuck at it for two years before I was brave enough to get out and look elsewhere.

LETTER TO MY MOTHER:

I didn't tell you any of my doings. I could no longer abide the pressure of those thumbs, and what got me out from under was a tin canoe. I saw one in a secondhand shop, going for thirty bob. Our house was in Mosman, on a hillside overlooking Chinaman's Beach and Middle Harbour, with its wonderful weekend flocks of sailing boats. How I loved to watch them. How I have always loved water, sea, surf. Ships, yachts, boats, enchanted me from afar. But thirty bob I could just scrape together, so I asked you about the canoe. Five minutes later when you had exhausted all your reasons why I couldn't possibly own such a thing, my mouth opened and out came the mild words, 'Well, I'm going to buy it.' And I was free.

My dear little canoe! Best thing I ever owned, just about. Sunday mornings, I'd be up and off, don bathing suit, rub over with coconut oil, grab some fruit and fags, and be down to the beach through the bush track. Drag little canoe across the sand to the shore, and Middle Harbour was mine, with its little coves and strips of sun-bakery sand, its rocks and clear bright water. Wouldn't come home till the south-easterly came up about 3 pm, and the labours of Sunday dinner were over. Couldn't stand all that ridiculous procedure, hours-long, and double if I had to cook it. I think that was when I gave up Sunday Dinners (mid-day) for ever.

Sometimes young nieces and nephews were allowed to come out with me, very special treat. Sometimes on a still hot night brother Bob might come – Oh how lovely to remember! Paddling along gently, quietly, the water deep, soft, dark, so dark that stars were reflected in the smooth swell of waves.

We had a bad time after that, you and I. I leaned a long way over backwards in my strike for independence; I needn't have been cruel. The thing to do on Friday nights was to go with a girlfriend into the city and do some late night shopping, have a meal in a coffee inn, and then go to film; or go to a 5 o'clock and have some food afterwards. I got to hate going home to dinner on Friday nights, and would stay in town by myself rather. I'm sure you thought I was doing something sinful, but, beast that I was being, I let you think what you would. But there's one thing I'm happy to remember. We had an unspoken pact. When you were going out somewhere, to play bridge, to a meeting, to church, you would ask me would I please be home on whenever it was, and I always would be, always. To do your hair, you're beautiful shining silver hair, crisp and wavy. You had a pretty little dark blue hat – I can see that hat! – with tiny flowers set across a kind of tuck in the front, and I'd arrange your hair with puffs over the ears and a swathe at the back, to make hair and hat one harmonious concoction. It was as though this pact was part of our real loving mother and daughter relationship, and the discord between us was an extraneous weed that just needed some master-gardener with one neat poke to dispose of it.

BOB AND IAN

Our mum had the normal standards of the times, I suppose, in some matters, but in others she was well and truly ahead of them. She believed in equal division of labour between the boys and girls in her family. We all had to take fair shares in household jobs. The only difference she allowed was that females do the ironing and males looked after the fires, though we could swap roles if necessary. Each made own bed and tidied own room, and we took turns in washing up. I forget what nights it was my turn, with my younger brothers Bob and Ian, but I don't forget the dodges they thought of for getting out of it (not that it was serious, just a good game). Ian had his girlfriend trained to ring him up at 7 o'clock, just the time dinner was over and the dishes piled up in the kitchen. He'd chat on for half an hour, expecting all to be done in that time. So Bob produced a counter trick – an urgent call to the toilet, where he'd stay for the duration of the phone call. There was only one thing left for me to do, so I'd nick out a book and have a read, and enjoy the sorry looks on their faces when they'd emerge and find everything waiting.

What a series of girlfriends Bob had! Ian had the one and only, then and forever after. He used to say to me, 'I can't understand the silly cow. What I reckon is, all girls have the same things, and when you've got one you like, why go to all that trouble chasing round the way he does.' But Bob would come home from a dance in the small hours, wake me up, and sit on my bed telling me all about the latest one. He said to me once, sometime much later, 'You know, sis, you once gave me a piece of very useful advice, one that I've always been grateful for.' 'Oh indeed,' I said, 'I wonder what that was?' 'You told me never to ask a girl if I could kiss her good night, just go ahead and do it.'

We used to have some fun in those days, though we didn't have much money. We three were the tail end of the family, all the others in good safe jobs or good safe marriages, or perhaps both. I was in my first job, Bob was a Law Clerk on ten bob a week, and Ian at university on a small allowance. The pair of them knew my paydays, every second Thursday, as well as I did, and after dinner they'd just mooch into my room and say, 'What about it?' We could get into the local 'flicks' for one-and-sixpence each, in the stalls, and walk there and back. On Sundays we can walk again to the Spit, across the bridge, and catch the Manly tram from there, thrippence each; the bus all the way from our place was ninepence – too much! Another sixpence to use the dressing sheds, and we'd surf all morning, sometimes the three of us all riding down on the same wave, yelling in ecstasy at one another. Sometimes, if we were all a bit flush, we'd walk again to the Spit and over the bridge, to a little riding school there, and hire horses for four bob each for the afternoon, and have lovely times riding through the bush of French's Forest.

In winter time our entertainment was even cheaper; it was free. We used to go rock-hopping from Chinaman's Beach round to Balmoral, great fun. Easy enough at low tide, but when it was high there were a few places where a good big jump was called for. Long-leggety beasties, both of them, and they'd zoom over. I'd be looking for a way round, but they'd say, 'Come on, you can do it, 'course you can,' so I did didn't I?

How lucky we were! That piece of Middle Harbour was as good as our very own. Sometimes we'd go walking and rock hopping the other way, down towards the Spit and then round the bushy hillsides and little bays back towards the Harbour itself. Sometimes on a calm night the full moon would call us out, rising into the sky and sending her brilliant path over the quiet water to the beach down there below us. On one such night we went right round to Grotto Point, just Bob and I. There, from the cliff top, we looked down on a rock pool of still, still water, and, perfectly reflected in it, the big round moon. Too much for Bob! He picked up a stone and threw it with all his might, thrilled with himself, dancing up and down on the rock – 'Look! I've smashed the moon!'

Another memory that belongs just to the two of us – coming home from a dance about three o'clock one soft summer morning, behold the morning star, low in the sky and huge, sending her own bright path across to us. Wonderful sight!

What a pair we were, Bob and I, for watching storms! There were two attic rooms in that wonderful house we had, and they looked straight out away to the Heads and the sea beyond. When we could see a storm coming, with great black clouds rolling in from the ocean, we'd climb out of the window and sit on the roof, again yelling in ecstasy as the tumult broke over us, with the rain pelting and drenching us through.

The joys of having brothers! The pleasures of being a sister! I even enjoyed it when I was pressed into the job of cutting Bob's hair. Whatever the price in those days, it was too much if a fellow had someone at home who had some barber's clippers and scissors – Oh how old they must be! I have them still. Our dad always cut the boys' hair when they were young, and when he was in his last illness, away in the Blue Mountains, he taught me, you might say, to use them and keep his own hair decently short. So they came to me after he died. Bob had a fine thick curly thatch of dark brown hair, and his lady-love of the moment liked my barbering, so I'd get to do it on Sunday mornings out on the side veranda. Though we got used to ticks, the first time I saw one I was startled – stuck into the back of his head, revealed in the pathway made as I ran the clippers up. After that we used to search ourselves for them when we came home through the bush, and douse them with kerosene, or stick them with a red hot needle point.

Needle! I trod on one once, standing upright in the carpet, and it broke and left half itself in my bare ball of foot. It had to be cut out and the wound stitched, and I had to go walking with a crutch and stick till it mended; and there came a wonderful wet stormy day, the sort of day that would call us away from book or desk. We'd look at one another and grin. Find some sandshoes, old coats, old hats, and be gone out, out into the lovely sweet rain and wild wind, trees tossing, waves whipping, the more the better –

and even on that day I remember, with the coat hanging over my crutch and tucked-up bandaged foot.

OLD BOSSES AND BLOKES

There's a well-known saying, 'Never introduce your donah to your pal,' but that's just what Julian did, and later Clarrie introduced me to Donald. He was a dear, kind man who would have been a steady and faithful husband, but – he didn't raise a flicker of fervour in me. He was a teacher and had a little car – rare luxury in those days. He had lots of friends, and there'd be great days with mobs of us on picnics to Palm Beach or National Park. He was so <u>good</u> to me, trying to do whatever I was keen on, like taking me to dances which he didn't enjoy, and once – once only ! – he took me to the ballet, which he hated. What he really liked was 'going to the pictures', and that was okay with me. Why did I have to meet good men like Donald, or else rapscallions like Brian!

He was a horror. I was a bit smitten with him, can't think why, except that he was my first sex encounter since Clarrie, though it was still a matter of fresh air and *coitus interruptus* (and only when it wasn't raining). But he did add something to my education. He was my first knowledge of an out-and-out gambler. He bet on all the horse race meetings, Wednesdays and Saturdays, and on the dogs too, and though he had a clerical job (which he disdained) he never had any money; but he was always talking about it, and his great wild schemes for making pots of it. He'd meet me after work to go to eat somewhere cheap enough, and then tell me I'd have to pay because he was broke. He'd even borrow a pound or two till payday. No kind of boyfriend at all. He came home with me just once. He and my mother couldn't abide one another, and he refused to come ever again. When we went out on Sundays for walks and rock-hops in places round the Harbour, he'd bring me home as far as the front gate and leave me there forlorn. Forlorn and raging with frustration.

Dear Donald was still there, in the background. He suffered the indignity of my going crazy over such a butterfly-chaser as Brian, and then gathered me in tenderly when that bit of nonsense was over. How happy he, his family, and my mum would have been if I had agreed to marry him. But I couldn't do it. He wanted himself a wife, so he found another girl to marry, and was a kind and loving husband to her all his life, which ended a few years ago. She and I are friends to this day.

I was twenty-five by now, and still floundering about – or as my mum would have it, 'not settled'. The second job I had was at least an improvement on the first.

The boss was a darling, and made me feel I was working with a friend rather than below a superior. He set me up in my confidence, and took the taste of the first boss out of my mouth, though in the years to come I would find the complex that man gave me rearing its still-ugly head whenever I started in a new job. This one did wonders for my dignity as a secretary and a person, and for my attractiveness as a female. Not that he made any advances, just was aware. It was the 2IC who used to pat my bottom as he went past. I was in a laboratory with a bunch of chemists, all male, who were testing gas appliances, and sometimes after work we'd drop into a pub for a beer – my introduction to this pleasant pastime. I did a good job and enjoyed working there.

Things were looking up all round, as I had a much more likely boyfriend by now too, a cheerful companion, enthusiastic in all the good times we shared. We went to dances, to the ballet, we'd hire horses and go riding. On summer Sundays we'd meet under the clock at Central Railway Station early in the morning, catch a train to Otley or Waterfall, hike through National Park down to a beautiful beach, spend a long, long day, and get back as late as we could. Moreover, he came home with me and Mother couldn't help liking him. We had a lot of fun, and this was a happy time in my life. But. First thing, my brain got restive after two years in that job (I must have been a two-year-stayer), and I set myself to do a course in Advertising, which is not a profession for which I entertain much regard. It just seemed something I could do that might get me moving on. Second thing, the affair became uncomfortable. The bloke didn't want to get involved to the marrying point because he was a Jew, and I just wasn't involved to that point anyway. So it seemed time to break the circle.

Those were the early days of girls saving up their money and going for trips abroad, and our architect sister, Winsome, had done this and was working in London. I wasn't as brave or as qualified as she was, and I decided to start off closer to home. Our sister Mary had married a New Zealander and was living in Wellington, busy about having her first baby. So, with her as a backstop, I resigned from my job, booked on the old *Awatea*, and away I went, February 1938. Got myself a job in an Advertising Agency, three pounds a week, and a 'room with cons', a pound a week, and felt myself pretty dashing.

It was a good time, that year in New Zealand. I didn't find the fellow I suppose I was looking for, who'd be a suitable husband for me. Made friends with a great girl who used to take me out into the country, walking mostly, at weekends. Used to love taking my lunch down onto the wharves, sitting in the sun and watching the ships. Was godmother to Susan when she arrived. Got to know my sister (ten years older than I) for the first time, and was able to help her through a tough time of illness. And for the first time, I actually enjoyed the work I was doing.

This boss was a good, fine person too. Gave me a job as part-time personal secretary, part-time copywriting 'as an experiment'. It worked well, and I got fun out of the writing part. He was delighted when his agency landed the account for publicity for the Labor Party when an election came up, although he was a Liberal supporter himself. He was properly in two minds about celebrating when Labor got in, kudos for the agency or sorrow for the ousted Opposition. At the end of the year I was in two minds myself; he offered me full-time advertising work with more pay, and I had a feeling towards going home to Sydney. Was it an instinct, was there something in the air? I can't remember that I was aware a war was coming, I hadn't ever been a person to follow world affairs. But anyway, it was a turn of fate (Lady Luck?). My heart was set on 5 pounds a week (big money!) and if he'd offered me that I'd have stayed. Four pounds ten, he suggested, and I went. Home again. It was the end of 1938.

I was living back in the bosom of my family, mostly broke and looking for jobs. I was months doing temporary work here and there, all of it unsatisfactory. The worst was in Woolworths, Head Office. That was an education! The atmosphere was one of frenzy, work, work, work, no second to waste, a whip at our backs all the time, not only the office girls but poor young buyers and heads of departments too. I marveled that these men were so young, and then realised that they would wear out early. The big typing room was on the sixth floor and would have had a splendid view over the city to the Harbour, but the bottom half of the windows were covered with white paint so we wouldn't be wasting time looking out. I think the award wage was £3.1.6, and as they paid us about two bob more, they thought they could drive us into the ground. Friday was late shopping night, and any Friday morning we could be told we would have to work late that night, and no way out of it. We daren't make ourselves a date for a Friday.

I was there for a few months when the Advertising course man found me another job, and it was like getting out of jail the Saturday morning I left that monstrous place.

Meanwhile I had gathered all my courage together, and told my mum that I wanted to move out into a flat of my own – so putting another crack in her poor heart. I was twenty-seven, and the time had really come. Lady Luck must have approved, because she helped me find a dear little flat close to Mosman wharf, where I had my own kitchen and bathroom, and, at my own discretion, my own double bed.

The new job sounded good. I was to be in charge of advertising in a firm that dealt with motor car sidelines. Four pounds a week. It was in a lovely office at the Quay, and the window next to my desk looked right over the water with the ferries bundling in and out. But the boss – he was truly a horror.

What was his name, the awful man? My job was mostly writing short pieces of copy lauding a car polish. He would never accept my gems as I handed them to him, but had to rant and rave and have them rewritten his way. We had one ridiculous argument, when he wanted me to start some screed with 'For upwards of twenty years …', and my pedantic mind thought there was no sense in 'for upwards of'. He had a boss complex of the first degree, and really liked to see his staff shivering in shoes. He was a much hated man. There was a story about the strictly-brought-up young man who had the job before I did, who used to come raging out of his office, plump down at his desk and swear furiously, *sotto voce*, for about ten minutes, and then get up and rush downstairs to the toilet, for the purpose of washing his mouth out with soap and water.

Of course it was a tense time, the middle of 1939, and if he was awful before the war started he was insufferable afterwards.

I only stuck it out till the end of the year.

3. On the Wrong Tack

My poor mother still had me in her womb, and it must have been one of the hardest things she ever had to bear, from her children, but I was living (no doubt a sinful life) in my own flat, away from home. It absolutely wasn't done in those days. Girls and women lived at home until they married. Nan did until she was 37, when she went to live at the small school 'for children of Christian Scientists' where she had been teaching since she got her hard-won degree. Mary also, till she was thirty-four, when she had her long service leave and her trip abroad, met Graham and married about a year later. Winsome, too, married in her late thirties. She was at home till she was twenty-nine, when she went to London and had a job for three years. After she came back naturally she lived at home— poor lady, I think now. Anyway, it was okay if the daughter was travelling or working overseas; that, mothers could be proud to talk about, but if she was in a flat on her own, in the same suburb even! Oh, shame!

As for my marriage, she couldn't help it, and neither could I. It was no ones 'fault', mistake that it was. She couldn't rest happy or sleep o'nights for wanting me to be wed. I think my siblings all wanted it too, they were fed up with me and my various blokes and bosses, and they were nearly all married or of marrying mind. I don't know why I felt the pressure and disapproval, I had made my break away and was living my own life, and only went home now and then. However, I must have. Was it helped, perhaps, because my job was just a stop-gap, and not a career I had any conviction about?

One evening as I was walking down Pitt Street to catch the ferry I bumped into Max, Bob's friend who had put me on the Advertising course. His mother was living in a remote suburb, he in a little room with cons. in the city, and a lonely life he was having. He walked me to the ferry, and a few days later I was surprised when he rang me at work and asked me to have dinner with him that evening. It turned out to be his 21st birthday. I was shocked that he could be so lonely in his life as to have no celebration of any kind in the pot for that day. He told me he'd been sitting at work and feeling a bit desolate, and he'd thought, 'What would I like best in the world?' So – he rang me. He used to sit at our meal table in Mosman, so he said, when Bob brought him home, and worship me from afar, thinking I was the most beautiful, wonderful, etc. etc. female he'd ever been near.

We went, I remember, to the downstairs (and inexpensive) dining room of the old Hotel Australia in Castlereagh Street, and had beer and curried lobster. Then we went to my little flat and played some records on the little windup gramophone, and so to the double bed and the start of our love affair.

At this stage, more than 40 years on, I sit and wonder why I said Yes when he asked me to marry him four weeks or so later. I had my independence at long last, with my flat and a 'good' job, even if awful, and I tossed it over my shoulder like a twirl of apple peel, like we used to in the game when we were kids. I wasn't marrying to get away from home, or for security – Max's salary was just the same as mine, four pounds a week. Of course I fancied I was in love, like many a one before and after me mistaking the half loaf for the whole bread, physical happiness for love itself, and I suppose that must have been it. Love of course meant marriage, all my life and all my literature telling me so.

But then, why oh why did we decide to be so pronto about it? And make the date for the deed within weeks? I can't think that the imminence of war had much influence over us, except for the tip-toe starting-block quality of the very air we breathed at that time. Even after it was declared, it was a long way off and there was no thought of blokes like Max enlisting and 'going to the Front'. I do know that Bob said to Max, 'You want to marry my sister? Then do it straight away before she changes her mind,' which I thought was in jest, but maybe Max took it seriously? Maybe? He must have. On my part it was an act of faith. This was Love, with a capital letter, and if he wanted me to prove it by promising before a parson, well then, I would.

LETTER TO MY MOTHER:

Dear Mother. It was impossible to explain this to you. I am only now explaining it to myself for one thing, and you and I were still at loggerheads. Much as you wanted me wedded, you didn't want it to be this mere boy (on four pounds a week), and above all, this rushing to the altar was anathema to you. The marrying of a daughter should have been happy, leisured business, with congratulations and rejoicings, engagement parties and kitchen teas, planning of occasion and designing of clothes. For you to be telling people in July that I was to be married in August was the swallowing of a bitter pill, and I suppose you dreaded that they would think there was a pregnant reason – if indeed you didn't think so yourself.

You invited us home to dinner in the hope of a good talk that would show us how you felt. You even spoke to Mr Hayley, our good family dentist since forever, hearing the news and saying, 'I didn't even know she was engaged'. Mr Hayley! Hecuba to me! We believed that if we wanted to be married, that was our affair entirely and no one else's. You tried with all your heart for a change of mind, but I was still in revolt against you, and paid no attention to your pain, or to your love either. Marriage we were set on, knowing nothing of each other except that we both loved music.

I honestly think I'd just have bowled along to a parson, in my one and only suit (black) that I wore to work every day, and had no fuss of any kind. But sister Winsome took me in hand, and we went shopping; she must have lent or given me some money, and she saw me fitted out with a beautiful dress, light coat, and a wonderful hat, all in navy blue and gold. She also rustled up a small party in my flat afterwards. It was two weeks before war was declared.

You wrote me a letter which I've kept among my treasures this long time because it summed up so perfectly the two sides of you, your love of the sentimental and dramatic, and your simple honesty. If I quote it here maybe I can now burn it.

'I should have dearly liked to have had you married from a little church here, and to have had those you love most, and those I love most, with us and Ian's dear ones too; but as I said, I could not manage to do it at such quick notice, in as sweet and loving a way as the only way in which I could do it. You and Ian have decided that your way is the one you can understand. There will be some extras you would like to have in your own way. The enclosed is with the love of your Daddy and Mummie.

                    Mother.

P.S. I am making you a wedding cake. Mum.

(enclosed was twenty pounds)

There's one more thing. After you died in 1958, sister Nan found a swag of diaries you'd kept over the years. Not knowing what to do with them, she sent me the one for 1939, in which you expressed all your frets and concerns over me at that time (which was almost too painful for me to read). And once the marriage was accomplished, cut, finish, not one more word of all that. You immediately switched to something else. I was a 'married woman' and had to dree my own weird. Even when we came to you, quite respectably in October, and said we 'had something to tell you', you wrote about it in a detached way – 'My little girl going to be a mother'.

HAVING MARRIED IN HASTE

No need to write a letter to my first husband. Time has rolled away the pain and bitterness, and there's no necessity now for anyone to forgive anyone for anything. We established a friendship long ago, and have danced together at three weddings, Jo's and his later two children's. But it was a sad time, the two years we stayed married (there it is again!), apart from the happiness and love our daughter Josephine brought us.

He had been an adopted child, and there was a sadness and bitterness at the bottom of him because of it – he used to say, 'I should never have been born' (because, he felt, his real mother didn't want him). He felt he really didn't belong anywhere, and how well I remember him saying to me (Oh indeed I remember!) 'You're so beautiful – and you're mine, you're <u>mine</u>!).

He suffered terribly from asthma when he was young, and would be sitting up in bed reading, reading, reading, while other kids of his age were out playing. This, I suppose, compounded his complex about being adopted, or at any rate didn't give it a chance to be rubbed away in the normal hurly-burly of childhood. His mother adopted the baby after her own husband was killed in the First World War, leaving her childless, and Ian was brought up by two women, his mother and his grandmother. We couldn't have had more different backgrounds!

We were different creatures in all our approaches to everything in life, except music, and no matter how I tried, and in how many ways I turned myself, I couldn't find a way to get the marriage working. I was up against 'the battle of the sexes', which was a new thing to me, and recrimination, tension and discord because of it I really didn't know how to handle. I was used to my brothers as men to live with, and to the simple understanding and acceptance of each other in the give-and-take of our family life; and I took for granted that marriage would be just like that, only more so; which of course it wasn't. Ian said to me once in a fury, 'It's a pity you couldn't have married one of your brothers!' Neither of us knew or understood what the other expected of marriage, or even what we expected to give and receive ourselves

— being married should all have been the waving of magic wands and living happily ever after.

It was in this time that I discovered what a cruel and destructive force sexual jealousy is; not in myself, but against me; and not for the present, but for love affairs of the past. Poor Ian would be seized by its mania at random, without any reason that I could see, seized and swept away beyond himself, for hours and days together, and then left totally contrite when the visitation was over. Each time both of us hoping never again. It was, I suppose, the worst effect of our difference in age.

We stumbled on for two years, when he decided to enlist, and was sent to the Middle East. After Japan entered the war and the Australian troops came back to Australia, we spent leaves together, but we never lived together again, and after the war was over and our names ultimately worked through the long, long list of matrimonial cases, we were divorced.

It was a glorious feeling, like a great sack of wet sand lifted off my shoulders, when it dawned on my muddled brain that I didn't have to go on struggling with the burden of non-understanding our marriage was. I could be free of it! I think I took the first step on my long road to personal freedom with that. One thing to say — I can guarantee an unhappy marriage as the ultimate self-confidence wrecker.

There's a big, big thank-you, though, to record. Four pounds a week we had to live on. Rent of a little house was 30 shillings, he kept 10 shillings for his lunches, fares and fags, so I had £2 to spin over all the rest. It was a scratch. And a simple life. God bless the choko and the junket tablet! There was a prolific vine all over our back fence, and choko was our green vegetable week after week, and a bowl of junket did its noble duty for dessert. But he must've scratched better than I. Somehow he kept on buying gramophone records, Beethoven and Mozart mostly, a few shillings at a time. He had a little pet music shop in Rowe Street, and when he'd go in on pay-days to pay off two bob on his last purchase, the music-shop lady would say, 'I've just got in something you'd love – Beethoven's Fourth Concerto with Geiseking – it's divine!' And he'd listen to the first side, find another two bob, and bring it home rejoicing. Hitler was running over Europe, the baby inside me was making me huge, and I was sitting, night after night, knitting and stitching, listening to great music. A sort of suspension of time, and of myself, but the music was real and abiding.

SHIPMATE AHOY!

It wasn't much trouble to me, having a baby; I was fit and fine, not even morning sickness coming my way. I did get quite huge, all poked out in front, with no extra fat on my thin arms or any other part of me, so I looked and felt odd and uncomfortable. The only small problem was, the baby was reluctant to emerge, and after being two weeks overdue, I told my doctor I was getting fed up. So he gave me an enormous dose of castor oil. This I immediately threw up, so he gave me another – and pronto! I went into hospital about six in the morning, and got on with the job. It was a Sunday – 'Sunday's child is bonny and blithe and good and gay'? So I hoped. Of course I had anaesthetic, it was normal procedure for those times, but only at the last. I was sitting up having roast chicken dinner by midday.

They kept me in hospital for two weeks – stuck in bed for ten whole days of it. What a load of nonsense! I was running round the place helping the nurses with little jobs after they let me get up. My only bother was a vast amount of milk. I'd never been greatly endowed as to breasts, and I couldn't get over the sight and sensation of having those great boobs on me. 'Mrs Bosom' the other mothers in my room called me. There was a woman in the next ward who wasn't having much luck trying to feed her undersized baby, and it kept crying all the time. A nurse came to my bedside one night, and said (hush, hush), 'Here, do you mind? I'm going to give the poor little thing a decent feed', and milked me like a cow for the purpose. I was glad to oblige. (Eight pounds four ounces my baby daughter was, nice and plump, with lots of black hair).

TO MY DAUGHTER

This is something that sticks in my gizzard to this day, and write it out of me I wish I could. That I was so stupid!

Before you were born I just took it for certain that you were a boy. I couldn't imagine myself with a daughter. I had no confidence with the mother/daughter relationship, the battles with my own mum so fresh in my mind. When I came out of the anaesthetic after the birth I looked up at the doctor, and realising it was all over, said, 'Oh … is he here?' 'He's here alright,' I heard, 'only he's a girl'. A little girl … a girl … how on earth was I going to get along with a girl? Such a beautiful little creature you were, and I loved you so desperately; here you were, not just an extension of two people's experience, but a whole life, a new person, here in my arms and in my charge and protection. I was demented; afraid to use my own nous, I fled to the Baby Clinic, giving you and myself over to the dogmas of the lunatic who was the current Prophet of the times, wretched man (it was a man), and may he roast in Hades till Kingdom Come.

Routine was his golden rule. Baby must be fed four-hourly, not a minute out either way. Demand feeding, as our mothers used to do, was worse than shameful, it was unspeakable. You could be crying with hunger at 5.45, and I almost crying with pain in my swollen breasts, but we had to wait till 6 o'clock precisely. Then of course the milk would spurt and you'd gollop it at a great rate; held at my shoulder and patted to get the wind up, you'd bring it nearly all up again in gouts down my back. I had a particular cardigan that I kept especially for feeding times, so that only one of my garments would be spoilt (which it was, wash I never so). The rules were absolutely rigid. Baby should put on exactly so many ounces a week, which you didn't, you poor little thing, as of course you weren't getting enough food – plenty waiting, but it didn't stay long. I dreaded our trips to the Clinic. Those nurses used to make me feel guilty and ashamed over your four ounces instead of the regulation six or whatever. Baby should take fifteen to twenty minutes at each breast, and you used to take about five, and nobody tried to work out the connection between my two sins.

After being fed, winded, and changed, you would be wrapped tightly in a bunny rug and put down in your cot. Pity help us if you cried. Picking up and cuddling was not allowed. 'It doesn't hurt baby to cry,' we silly mothers were told, 'so long as you're sure he's dry and hasn't any wind.' ('Baby' was always called 'he' by this

Prophet, his followers and his literature. Don't I just wonder how many babies he had!) You'd cry and cry and I'd leave you crying in your cot, memory makes it for hours. I hope it wasn't. A bit of cuddle and love we were allowed, just once a day before the 6 pm feed, in what was dictated as 'the mothering hour'. And that was the only time grannies and aunties could get a cuddle too, never Oh never at any old time of the day. Not good for Baby, all that picking up and fussing!

Very soon came the potty training, long before you could sit up, with my holding you over a pot after every feed, and greeting a dribble of widdle with joyful cries of 'That's a good girl!' Between six and nine months of age was the time scheduled for weaning baby, beginning with a slap of Farex at one feed and a slurp of cod liver oil at another – which made a rich addendum to the goo on the back of the poor old cardigan. But I struck trouble because my super-abundant supply of milk began to dwindle away, from lack of the good long twenty minutes haul of stimulation; so you had to have a supplementary bottle, and you wouldn't have a bar of that; so 'they' decided I must wean you entirely, and at once. Bottle or nothing for you! Pain in the breasts for me. It was torture. I could think of nothing but mixtures of milk, ounces of milk and ounces of infant, for weeks together … Oh, I can't bear to remember it, let alone write about it. I was in despair because you wouldn't have a bar of your orange juice either, and I had to be told, *told* that grape juice would do as well. I have never been such a fool in all my life. Once a week I'd take you to the clinic, and let the rigid acolytes of the Great Prophet propound his cruel religion, to our mutual misery. Physically we survived it, and emotionally too, in the long run.

You always were a quiet little person, didn't speak a word till you were two, and from a small thing, the stronger your emotion the less you were able to utter. When you were at Nan's school, and I'd come for you on Friday evenings, you'd come running down the path and clutch me by the knees, beaming with joy, but dumb. We'd have huggings and kissings, but not a word would come over your lips for an hour or more. Growing up, you could never tell me what you were thinking and feeling, not even in the traditional heart-to-heart time, over the washing up. I still don't know if you've ever felt you wanted to. When I think back, no wonder! Poor little child, you were always left alone, alone in bassinette, alone in cot, alone in playpen. No wonder your generation has taken a complete *bouleversée*, and chucked all those inhuman rules well and truly overboard.

However, it can, now and then, occur to grannies of my generation to wonder if you had to lean quite so far over backwards – to throw the baby out with the bath water as it were. What a fine old rod you're putting in pickle for yourselves, we think, you and the Nursing Mothers, with your faith in giving baby the breast whenever he/she wants it, and until baby decides he/she wants it no more. We've seen some of you with two-year-olds, and you can't go off and leave them in some kind of care for so much as one day or night. Perhaps it's pickling the rod for us grannies that we're bothered about. There comes to stay the little one (weaned at last) who has ever been allowed to make his/her own his decisions about when and what he/she will eat, when be bathed, go to bed, get up, when play and with what, and poor grannie's household is utterly upwumbled, while she simply can't see the difference between this and her own anathema –'letting the kid have its own way all the time'. And her floor is prickling with miniscule bits of plastic, wood, felt, cardboard; and worst of all, pieces of those damned educational toys which have to be fitted into something, or each other. It'd be nice, we think, if the little one had a smidgin of – and bugbear to your lot though it be, I'll write the word – discipline.

(The week before Christmas I meet her in the shops, the grannie with her shopping basket heaped high, an air of great import and busyness about her. I greet her and ask, 'The children coming for Christmas?', and she answers me with a supremely smug smile, which is saying to me, 'My four beautiful and lovely grandchildren are coming, and I have done all the preparing and cooking and am just finishing off my shopping.' A week or so later I see her and the dazzle has gone out of her. She looks as though her feet are hurting and she could do with a good lie down. I greet her and ask, 'The children gone?' She gives a big sigh and says 'Yes', and I wait for it, and it comes, 'Nice to see them come and nice to see them go.')

4. Backwash of the War

{Ed. Six pages are missing here from the original typescript}

… I could possibly have had. And I learned to drop everything else and be sitting at the piano by 2pm regardless. This helps me now when I'm writing. I can be sitting in front of the typewriter when my self-set time arrives, no matter what the undone domesticities. But it was bad luck I had no access to a piano when we came back to Sydney, and I played no more.

LITTLE LETTER TO LADY LUCK

I'm not writing to the kind of lady who might be a fairy who goes to christenings and bestows gifts of more or less goodness. No, to random, gratuitous, promiscuous old Lady Luck, we never know where you are or what you're about, but now and then you decide it's time you paid us a visit.

The first big job you did for me was in 1928 when I left school, and my dad refused paying my way through university if I could get a Teachers College Scholarship and be paid for. He dismissed my protests that I didn't want to be a teacher as though I hadn't uttered them, likewise my dread of the three-year bond that went along with the scholarship. We got an application form and he supervised my filling it out, then he turned the form over, and while I blushed all through with shame he listed on the back the scholastic achievements of my older siblings. When the results came out I had the scholarship I didn't want. But there was another result to come, the Exhibitions as they were called, the free places. Dad would have been content with one of those. It was part of his credo and had nothing to do with his income, that we should earn something towards the cost of our tertiary education. I had a middling sort of pass and didn't think I had a hope, but you stepped in, dear Lady Luck, and gave me the pleasure of declining that horrible scholarship, and going to the university 'unbonded'.

Now in my story comes 1943, wartime, and I am back in Sydney looking for a job. I started off in a solicitor's office, and one Saturday morning in the tram taking me to town, you turned a right blast on me. You kept telling and telling me to buy a newspaper and look in the Positions Vacant columns; I kept forgetting and you kept on nudging till I did. And there it was. The advertisement that said, 'Here, young Barbara, this is for you'. A stenographer/graduate wanted, as secretary to an Australian Army Education Committee. I sat me down and typed out an application with great care. I laughed as I did it and I laugh again now to remember, I appended a list of the family's scholastic achievements. I wanted that job. I wonder if you were still nudging me? Next came the interview, a most impressive do, in the evening, with four imposing gentlemen sitting in a board room at a vast table, with pens and folders in front of them, questioning me at length. But I was cheerful enough – I could feel you right beside me, Lady Luck. One of the gentleman said that part of the job would be persuading chaps perhaps reluctant to produce reports on army education activities, and how would I go about that? You made me give a grin and say, 'Part begging, part bullying, and the rest kidstakes,' and I reckon it was that answer that tipped the scales and got me the job. Or was it when one of them looked at my appendage, and said something like, 'Gosh, that's some record! Ten in the family, seven degrees and three diplomas!'

Nine pounds a week make me feel quite affluent, but it was a fringe benefit — I was back in my own basket, among people of my own kind, though they were something more accomplished than I was, being professors, lecturers, historians, Heads of Commissions — very prestigious persons. But we used the same kind of language and understood one another. Also I think they liked me. I certainly enjoyed knowing them, and doing a good job of what they wanted done. Inside their requirements I had a fine and dignified independence, which finished off the job that working with Nan at Baulkham Hills had started, and at long, long last my confidence in myself was established, packed tight and even running over.

A great friend of mine in later years used to talk about 'un-work' and 'non-work'. Un-work was futile nothingness, as if to pile up stones in one place and then for no purpose to hoist them to another. Non-work was doing something that had all the semblance of work, but in fact had no sensible or useful result, which was what that job was. I'd go to meetings, Committee and Subcommittee, and take down the Minutes of proceedings, type them up, duplicate and circulate them, all about the ways where these prestigious scholar fellows could help the education officers to do their jobs. 'The crackling of thorns under a pot'. Another way to put it would be, 'It was a wartime job and seemed like a good idea at the time'. It lasted just under two years (once again!), and packed itself up in 1945 when the end of the war was clear to be seen close ahead. My thanks to you anyway, Lady Luck. You don't often visit me, but you make a proper job of it when you do.

RITA

I was still married, of course. Ian and I had agreed that the best thing to do with our marriage was to end it. Divorce couldn't be got when the man was away on active service, and unhappy marriages just had to wait till the war would be over and the servicemen home again. Lady Luck had gone with the wind, and wasn't helping me at all in finding a place to live. I had a room, with shared cons., in the flat of a businesswoman who had a terrible habit – she never turned the blaring racket of her radio off, whether she was in or out, asleep or awake. Then I shared a flat with a soldier's wife for a while, and at last I shared a house in Maroubra with Rita, who had a job with the American Forces.

It was a lovely big house, looking out to sea, and I had the use of three rooms at the back, and shared the kitchen and bathroom. Very pleasant, but it was a devil to get to. There was a bus that passed the corner of the street in peak hours, but if I was going home at night there'd be a Randwick tram to 'Peter's Corner', and then a long walk. Collecting Jo from school and taking her back at weekends was an ordeal of connecting buses. But I had to be grateful for what I could get.

Rita was good fun, and a kind soul to me and to Jo. We had lots of laughs, but I remember her particularly because she was afraid; afraid for her person, catching diseases from public toilet seats for instance, or from handrails in buses (she never went anywhere without gloves on); afraid of her house and possessions being got at, so that, all else secured, even her bedroom door was locked when she was out. This was extremely aggravating to me, as the telephone was in that room.

One time I came home with Jo on a Saturday afternoon, and didn't have my key. Rita wasn't due back for hours, and I was quite stonkered facing that utterly locked-up house. At last I thought me of the hatch into the kitchen designed for milk and bread deliveries, and worked out that if I could find something to stand on for a start, I could just squeeze my body through it. With considerable wriggling and kicking, this I did. I was fool enough to tell Rita about it, and she was beside herself with distress. If I could get in that way, so could the Big Bad Bogey Man she was so afraid of! (He'd have to have been a skinny one!). The hatch was made impregnable forthwith, and I learnt my lesson about the key.

Through all this Rita revealed something to me. She was alone in the world, had had a disastrous sort of non-marriage and had now no husband or child, no father, mother, uncle, aunt, or any kind of relation at all. I couldn't believe it possible, couldn't get my thoughts round to imagining what it must be like, I who belonged in such a mob. My father one of six, my mother one of nine, and I one of ten. I had uncles, aunts and cousins laid on, even some whom I'd never met. I had a grand wide pick of people to call on in times of stress, and Rita had not a single solitary one. This helped me to understand her fears, and gave me to think about my lack of them; and I realised that I'm an incurable optimist, and not afraid of 'what might happen', for another reason beyond my natural cheerfulness and my sense of belonging in a family, and that is my teaching in the faith of Christian Science. Though long, long abandoned, they engendered a habit of thought that I suppose is with me still. You couldn't be afraid of sickness because any ailment of the body was only an error of thinking; even if you were, that is seemed to be, ill, what you had to do was know the truth (you had to be good at it) and errors would disappear. And the truth was: 'The only reality is God, Spirit, Immortal Truth, Infinite Mind. There is no reality in matter, which is mortal error. Man is the Image and Likeness of God, so he is spiritual, perfect, and eternal.'

'Give me a child until he is seven ...' – I had this until I discarded it at eighteen. So always, still, if I land in trouble – illness, unhappiness – what really bothers me is: there must be a way out, where and what is it? There have been some bad patches in my life. Not physical ones. There was a Good Fairy at my christening, that's for sure, and I've never been ill beyond the stuff kids get, a couple of rip-roaring 'flus, and a weird throat wog that got me in Bahrain or somewhere on a flight home from England one time. But I've been stuck in unhappy doldrums, of bitter memory, in the course of seventy-odd years, and they've always been double. One, because I was in them, and two, because I knew there had to be a way out and it was up to me to find it.

That makes me think about another thing about the Christian Science upbringing. If you did have a gut-ache or whatever, you kept it to yourself. It was nothing to talk about. If you were smitten severely enough for taking to your bed, you'd confess, with profound apologies. But whether this was because of the Christian Science, or just from the disgrace of being a nuisance in a big family, I'm not exactly clear at this stage. However, it was definitely so, and I am, and always will be, not only bored but slightly offended by a tale of aches and pains, pills and potions, and what the doctor said.

However, I should thank my afraid friend of years ago for the exercise of sorting this all out in my mind.

LETTER TO A LIEUTENANT

While I was living with Rita and working for the Army Education lot, I was friends with a Warrant Officer in the Sydney L of C called Sam, and his wife Jean. Into my office they came one afternoon, in cheerful and cheeky mood after a lengthy and very liquid luncheon. 'Come on,' they said, 'Come on out and have a drink with us.' 'Go away,' said I, 'I'm a working woman and have some Minutes to type.' 'Rats,' they said, 'you can do it tomorrow, and we've got two fellows downstairs waiting for us – we need you to help us entertain them – we promised them we'd collect you. Come ON.'

We went to the lounge of the old Australia Hotel in Castlereagh Street, and the beer being 'off' till 5 pm, we drank some purple-coloured cocktails called 'Parfait d'Amour' – ouch! Sam, Jean, a very young and handsome private called Steve, and a not-so-young or handsome (but fair enough) Lieutenant called Whit. You. To whom I've been married now for over thirty years. We had a bright and gay time, especially after the beer came on, and we had some dinner in the old Aarons pub where we had to queue up for the dining room, as was wont in war time. Somehow we acquired one whole bottle of very crook sherry, and went to

Sam and Jean's flat to discuss it and a few other things, along with lots of laughter. I think Steve melted away, and I'm sure I finished the evening resisting your rather inebriated and very cheerful attempts to seduce me. Not that I had any objection other than a feeling I had taken a liking to you, and didn't want a here-today-gone-tomorrow business.

I did get the Minutes typed the next morning, and in the afternoon it was all to do again as before, Sam and Jean arriving and coercing me, the drinks, the dinner, the return to the flat, and there was no resisting this time. It was a matter of mutual combustion; and I had a feeling that you had taken a bit of a liking to me too. You told me, much later, that I shook you a little by saying afterwards, 'I needed that.' Bold baggage Barbara? It was true, what harm to say it?

Next day your leave was over and you were away to camp at Greta. You said you'd write to me. Would you? Was it just a war-time flash in the pan? The very air in the Sydney streets, pubs, restaurants and cafes was flashing with sexual excitement, servicemen with girls on or in their arms everywhere, as if singing 'eat, drink and be merry – gather ye rosebuds – roll out the barrel – roll me over in the clover'. But, there was this feeling I had.

You did write a little note, making a date on your next leave. I met you at Aarons pub. I'd been in a state of dither all day, and when I saw you and we grasped hands, the dither vanished into plain happiness. So we drank and dined, and then back to my place at Rita's. We listened to some music – Tchaikovsky's First Piano Concerto – a war-time craze) – and then our urgency took us over. You picked me up, you did, you did, and carried me into the bedroom, treading on a record lying on the floor as we went (bad luck, as I had it on loan from the L of C, and I had a terrible time later on to replace it). We didn't bother about it then! We were gone a million.

You had to do the long walk to Peter's Corner for a taxi at whatever hour in the morning, poor bloke. You were to come the next afternoon, Saturday. I sat on Rita's front steps looking out over the ocean, waiting for you, and being most uncomfortable, oppressed with a feeling that my destiny had caught up with me, and I wasn't quite ready to receive it with open arms. Were you with me, Lady Luck, or agin me?

We were well and truly in love, deep seas over. There was a short leave, like a crazy ecstatic dream, and then you were whizzed away to New Guinea.

You gave me a ring, at least you gave me the money and I bought it (Oh portent of things to come in thirty years of birthdays!), a biggish opal set in hand-wrought gold, which suited my big hand – suits, indeed. We wrote swags of letters. My great moment of the day was coming home to the letter box, and crushed to the earth was I if no letter for me. I lived in my thinking and dreaming about you. For heaven's sake, I was thirty-three and had no more sense than I had at twenty-seven. I made you up into everything I wanted a man to be – intelligent, charming, full of gaiety and humour and appreciation of life's good gifts, and above all, aware and understanding of other people, loving, kind and generous in your approach to the world's inhabitants and problems. I don't know even yet what you made me up into; I wasn't it, but you loved it, whatever it was.

As ever, I was impressed by myself having such intense feeling, and I let it have its head. This was Love with a gorgeous capital illuminated letter, and when the war was over Love would find a way, no need to be concerned about mere ephemeral blocks such as my having a husband, a child now five, and your getting back to civilian life – that capital letter Love would fix all that in no time flat.

Which it didn't. Came the end of the war some eighteen months later (and the end of my fine job). In due course, October 1945, you were flown home, and straight to Melbourne where you lived. And crash, bang, wallop, thump, crump, stop. 'Not a drum was heard, not a funeral note' – no letter, no phone call, no telegram, nothing. After weeks there was one remote sort of letter, telling me that you thought it a 'fair go' to keep out of the picture till Ian should come back, and then no more. So there I was, I and my love hanging around in space.

5. Finding Direction

I battled with it for a while before I accepted it. Wrote letters that got me no answer, cried and carried on, at last even went to Melbourne because I just had to find out, which I did, and fool I that I hadn't seen it coming, or worked it out for myself. Dreams over, back to real life. Those years in the army were a state of suspended animation in a man's personal life – all to do was do as one's told. Whit was nearly forty and had to gather himself together. Back to work as a teacher, and with a new sense of responsibility to life in general, better he get his degree. So a part-time training course and part-time teaching. As for Barbara, she couldn't be coped with at all. She had a husband, no longer ephemeral, but a solid, cold, hard fact of a husband. She was part of the wartime dream, lovely but gone with the painful stark light of day.

So. I had to start again, all roads round. Find a job, and, as I had left Rita, a place to live, and get going. It was a funny year. Did I have four different jobs, or five? I'd take any secretarial job that was going – one awful one was in a big insurance office – and stick it till I could no longer. Then try again. Couldn't get back into my basket nohow, but I had to get some money at the end of the week and at least pay my rent and my daughter's school fees. But there's another big thank-you to record. While Ian was in the army I of course was drawing a Private's wife's pay, such as it was. After he came back into civilian life, and we agreed that our ways were irrevocably parted, he made me an allowance for his daughter. He didn't have much to spare, but he never failed in sending it, for years, right up to the time he found a new spouse, which was two or three years after I did.

As for now, 1946, though I had told him that Ian had had his 'fair go' and there was no reconciliation, Whit the Lieutenant was gone out of my life, doing whatever he was doing away there in Melbourne.

At least Lady Luck decided to produce a bit of compensation, and found me a splendid place to live, with a delightful character, Mrs Lees. Rose her name was, and her husband was Perc. The two of them ran a bed and breakfast guest house in Vaucluse – glory, glory, glory, what a spot it was in! On top of the hill, next to the water tower. Look out of the front windows over some gardens, and the Harbour lay like a magic fairytale carpet at our feet. Look out of the back windows over a stretch of streets and houses, and there was a great wide blue of ocean. Me and my sea and Harbour – there I was again! I couldn't believe my luck when I was able to get a room with her, even though she gave us only breakfasts and we had to find lunches and dinners where we might. Seven guests she had, and she did love to know about us all, specially our romances, boyfriends, girlfriends, love affairs, carryings on, high jinks if any, the higher the better. She'd be in her sitting room in the evenings, and would hear the front door open and close. 'Is that you?' we'd hear. 'Come in and have a cigarette.' In other words, 'Come in and tell.'

LETTER TO MRS LEES

I don't know who had the more fun, you out of us or us out of you. You were a Jewess, small, dark and volatile; Perc. was a gentile, tall, thin and fair; you bossed the socks off him. You'd cook the breakfasts, and have each one on a tray ready for the time we'd agreed on, and darling Perc. would bring them up to our rooms. He would knock and then bring in the tray; if I might be still asleep, he'd stand there and chat on about the weather and news until he was quite certain I was properly awake. Then there'd be your great yell from the kitchen downstairs, 'Perc.!', and his meek reply 'Coming my love.' All of us who ever stayed there would remember your getting very scotty with him over something, and scolding him, 'Oh Perc, go to hell!', and his gentle answer, 'All in God's good time, my love.'

A fine thing about your house was that it was close to Nan's school, and I could pick up my daughter after work on Fridays and we'd walk round. You didn't mind having a little child there at weekends, found me a mattress and she used to sleep on the floor. She'd wake up early and come into my bed, where she'd find an apple perhaps and a book under the pillow, and would read in great content till Perc. brought in our breakfasts; but Perc used to get very cross with me for lying there asleep and 'neglecting' my child.

If I ordered it and paid two bob extra, you'd cook us a dinner on Saturday, midday. What a dinner! Your old stove wasn't too good for baking, so it was always boiled meat, corned beef or pumped lamb, and there's be potatoes, pumpkin, onions and cauliflower in white sauce, beans, carrots, Oh such a piled up plateful. Jo and I used to have one between us for lunch, and save the other for tea – heat it up in your kitchen, or have it cold. Dinners, generally, were a haphazard business, but no matter. I used to buy brown bread, butter and sardines on Fridays, and Jo, long since fed, would have a second tea with me. I knew all the fair-enough cafes where I could get me week-day dinners, round about Rose Bay and Vaucluse – I haven't been there for over thirty years, and what of them now I wonder? Sometimes I settled for grapes and apples, munched over a book.

I'll put in a letter to my daughter just here about that time in Vaucluse. It was a happy time, I think now, looking back, happy for some things anyway, though we didn't have a home and a settled pattern of life, or a foreseeable future. Ian had gone to Melbourne to live, there was nothing doing in the divorce line, and I was still in the process of grieving about, and trying to get over, that bygone Lieutenant. My daughter was the core of my life.

LETTER TO JO

My weekends were entirely given to you. Summer time was lovely. We could walk from the guest house down to Neilsen Park – in fact we started that on sunny Spring days, going along by the Vaucluse gardens all abloom and wafting the sweet strong perfume of stocks. Down at the beach I'd lie on the sand and go to sleep in the sun, and you'd be perfectly happy on your own with the two best playthings in the world – sand and water. Sometimes we had another child or two with us, little 'left-at-schools' when parents couldn't come. There were two sisters who often came –what were their names? Cousins, many times;

Chalice, and Harry the year he was with Nan. Though the war was over, toys and playthings were still not being made. I did manage to find a water-wing contraption in a Disposals store, navy blue canvas with a strap around the body and two inflatable pouches at the sides, and you started learning to swim by dog-paddling around the pool with me.

Winter time we managed something, maybe a trip to the Zoo or just a ride around the Harbour on a ferry. What a quiet little girl you always were. You didn't talk much, seemed quite happy just to be with your mum, enjoying, say, the beauty of the colours of rocks and foreshores reflected in the calm water of Mosman Bay. Always had a capacity of living in your own mind and imagination. Almost never asked me for anything. Though once you did beseech me to take you to the Show. The Show! I think all the other kids must have talked about going. So we went. And you begged for a show doll on a stick. I reckoned they cost too much for the bit of doll and scrap of tulle that they were. You looked up at me with serious face and said, 'But I can get a ton of fun out of just one doll.' And you won. 'That's true,' I said, 'so you can'.

There wasn't much going by way of entertainment. I don't recollect ever taking you to the pictures – perhaps films for kids weren't being made. Once we went to some fascinating Indian dancers. Once to the Bodenweiser Ballet's children's matinee. First time you'd ever seen ballet. I even remember that it was *The Frog Prince*. You went into a high state of enchantment; just sat spellbound. When it was over and we stood up to go, you didn't say a word but tugged my hand and just pulled me down towards the curtain with irresistible compulsion. We went through the door and behind stage (I knew some of the dancers, and Madame, as I used to go to her classes for recreation – I was no dancer). You stood, still silent, till all the costumes were off, the set dismantled, and the last bit of magic was all packed away. Then a sigh, a tug of the hand, and we could go.

At the end of the year there were school concerts, and you had parts in the lovely plays that Nan wrote. The one I especially remember was at the end of 1945, so you were only five – truly? The concert was in the form of a story-ballet, and you were chosen to be the princess; the blond Terry was the prince. I had to make your dress, to Nan's precise specifications, which somehow I accomplished within the confines of my room at the guest house (I did have my sewing machine). It was pale blue, ankle length, with little white puff sleeves and big blue flowers stitched onto the skirt. Your dark hair was put in rags the night before, so you had pretty long curls, and a proper picture you were. And a proper lovely job you did of your part. You were gone away entirely, a fairy princess, not Jo at all. Nan told me of how, that evening after tea and the dusk falling on a damp, misty night, she missed you, and looking from the back veranda down the bank to the tennis court, where the concert had been, she saw you, little creature on your own, still bewitched, dancing the whole story through again.

It's interesting to think that these memories, which stand out clear and vivid pictures for me, are probably all vague and smudged together for you, if you have them at all. Do you even remember Mrs Lees?

She was all kindness to you. What of the time you got the measles? Poor sick little child, you had such a dose, and I had to have you away from school and in my care. Time off from work, okay, but what about my landlady? I was still sore with the memory of Rita, my frightened friend, the time when you had the chicken-pox, and she couldn't bear to have you in the house – it might as well have been the plague. So I tried to keep it from Mrs Lees. Pulled down the blinds and said you had 'a bit of a fever'.

She brought you everything possible to think of by way of junket and jellies and milk shakes, and fed me as well over that time, and wouldn't take any extra money. So concerned she was – and beside herself with curiosity. So of course the day came when she got a good look at you, and said 'It's the measles! She's got the measles!' – and was just kinder than ever. No fear of catchings or any dire consequences.

But again, in spite of her open-mindedness and woman-of-the-worldness, she had an unexpected streak of the old-fashioned. She came into my room one evening for a chat, and I was reading to you. I'd got my hands on a really good little book about the facts of life, and we were engrossed. 'What's that you're reading?', says she. 'It's a book about where babies come from,' says you. 'Oh,' says she, 'and where did you come from? A cabbage patch?' I can see your face and the happiness in it as you said softly, 'I came from Mummy.' And I can see the shock and horror in her face, and hear her voice saying, 'But that's absolutely disgusting, reading that to a child!'

One thing I was determined on was that you'd get this information in a simple and natural way. I wonder if I ever told you how my own mum imparted it to me? As I was the youngest of five daughters, she must have had enough practice in the essential 'little talk' to feel she had got it down to a fine art. And she told me that 'if a man managed to impregnate me with his organ,' I would have a baby. I was as innocent as the dewy morning, and when the little talk was over I made for the dictionary. All I knew was that there was a word printed on matchboxes, 'impregnated', and I didn't know whatever that meant; and as for 'organ', I had to read through about half a page of fine print in the big Webster's before I found out what sort of organ she was talking about. Certainly the whole doings didn't appear to be much fun, and I held the notion for some years that a lady gritted her teeth on a wedding night and went through with the performance, once, and then she was impregnated for ever after.

WELL-CONSIDERED MARRIAGE

I lived with Mrs Lees for over three years, and the other guests kept changing. Some were less sociable than others, but the friendliness of the establishment usually won people over.

There was one woman who had the little downstairs room next to the front door for a short time, who had Mrs Lees mystified. She was a charming person, in her forties perhaps, well-dressed and pretty, recently separated from her husband and addicted to the bottle. We never knew when she would knock on our doors and waft in, quite nicely inebriated, settle herself for some wafty conversation, and then waft away. What had Mrs Lees beat was, one, where she got her supplies, and two, where Oh where in her room did she hide them? Mrs Lees used to do out the whole place every day, and she told me she'd searched every corner of the lonely lady's room and couldn't find the secret. Sober at six o'clock and drunk by eight, and Mrs Lees never worked it out.

We had a happy little custom of collecting together in someone's room or other, supposing someone had got hands on a bottle of grog; rum was the easiest to come by, and we'd drink it with lemon squash. Mrs Lees always seemed to be available for these cheerful occasions, but never Perc. We must have been too frivolous for him.

I'd been there for about a year, in this job and that, and I had just landed into the one that kept me busy for the next – yes, two years. It was a hot, still night in January, the sky soft and dark and spangled with stars; the Harbour soft and dark too, and spangled with lights. Some five or six of us were together in Bette's room, enjoying a bottle of something and each other's company, when suddenly there was a fellow standing in the open doorway.

'What do you want?' said Mrs Lees.

'Who're you?' said Bette.

And 'Oh,' I said, though hard to believe my eyes, 'it's a friend of mine'. It was my ex-lieutenant. Twelve months incommunicado, come to Sydney on some spur to see his nephew, the handsome young private mentioned before, and to see me, perhaps.

Wretch. I had thought that fire was just about out, and there it was, straight away flaring up again, and upwumbling me. It was a short spasm, our bodies as urgent as ever, but my heart had a reserve of caution. Just as well. He was soon off and away, and I didn't see him again for – have a guess – two years.

I was still married. No divorce could ever have taken as long as ours did. Our names reached the top of the list in 1947, but the case was withdrawn because of a blunder in the petition; so there was nothing left but a three-year desertion suit and the bottom of the list again. In those days divorce was treated as a punishment against a guilty party. If I had been wicked my spouse could sue on those grounds, and if proven, I would be divorced to punish me. Bad luck if he confessed to having been wicked himself – no one guilty party, no suit, no divorce.

I stayed in the B&B apartment with the gorgeous view, and drew a good salary doing more non-work, this time as a research assistant with the Film Division of the Department of Information. It was a full and hectic two years, but I don't feel any need to write about them. Over my life I could think of events in the way my friend thought of work. An un-happening is a futile nothingness that comes along in spite of yourself, and really has nothing to do with you. A non-happening seems to be important, and painful or joyful at the time, but looking back on it you can see it added nothing to your life and your journey. (I know the expression 'non-event' is common these days, but that to me means a fizzer, something that didn't turn out.) Those years were full of non-happenings. I met some interesting characters, made a couple of good friends, and had some fun – mainly collecting in a pub after work and talk-talking over a beer or two. But I honestly cannot remember one piece of useful work I did in those years, or one thing that abides with me to this time.

It was towards the end of 1948 that I sat down and wrote a letter to the ex-lieutenant. I still thought my feeling for him had been a genuine one, and his for me too, and I was tired of a complicated non-relationship I had been in. It was as though I felt 'Enough of all this non-life. It's time we got on with real living.' He wrote back. He came to Sydney at the end of the year (his degree accomplished), and we combusted again, as ever only more so. We got together after that whenever we could – long weekends, Easter, he to Sydney, I to Melbourne. It was clear that something had to be done about it; the time had really come. I left my job, Mrs Lees, and Sydney in May the next year; packed up myself and my daughter and went to Melbourne. Quite mad. Stark raving crazy.

Of course I had a difficult and unsettled time there in temporary jobs and places of abode, till the end of the year, when Whit got an appointment to Mildura. We decided to burn our boats and go there as married, hoping for the divorce to come through within months anyway. We reckoned the only way we could carry it off was to pretend that we had had a wedding. I'd gone off with Jo to Sydney to stay with Nan and Mother in the Christmas holidays, and he came to join us, got on his bike to ride from Melbourne – took him five days, what with some lifts on the way.

The family hadn't met him, and Nan took to him on the spot when she saw this sunburnt sweating man wheeling his bike up her front path. Mother was more cautious, but it was clear she'd come his way when, a little later on, she was heard to announce, 'I'll say this for Whit, he hasn't got a lazy bone in his body.'

We set up the date, bought a ring, sent telegrams to family and friends, went to dinner to celebrate, and almost convinced ourselves.

And here I must say some thank-yous to brother Ian and his wife Betty, not long back from New Zealand, where they'd been living for some years. When I was desperate for somewhere to live in Melbourne, they shared their house and their lives with Jo and me, and with Whit too, a lot of the time. I don't know how they put up with us, it wasn't exactly an easy situation, but we all survived as good friends.

To Nan, as always and forever unselfish and accepting. I think it put a crack in her heart when I took Jo away from her school and her T.L.C., all for so vague a future, but she made no weep and wail or word of condemnation, and did her best to condone the pretend wedding with a generous gift. It's strange that I can't remember Mother's reaction, or anything about my brothers and sisters – perhaps they just washed their hands of me.

To Whit's family, especially his poor little mum who must have had more than a crack in her heart when all her dreams for her one and only best beloved son to end in a wedding that wasn't. They got together and decided what each would give – linen, cutlery, a pressure cooker – and put on the act as best they could, to themselves and their near and dear, that we were in fact married. Bless them.

6. Billowing Sails and Blithe Passage

It was a brave enough thing to do in 1950, pretend to be married when we weren't and always with the chance that the divorce wouldn't eventuate; but braver for Whit than for me; his job would have gone sky high if it had become known. I didn't feel brave, I just felt married. When, at last, the divorce did come through during the year, we couldn't confess ourselves by trotting down to the local registry office, so we waited till we went to Sydney in the Christmas holidays. A strange feeling for me, to be making vows and marrying when I'd been Mrs Whitley for a whole year.

LETTER TO MY LOVE

Our halcyon days. I can see them now through a bright mist of happiness. It's interesting to look back and sort out what was of abiding importance, and interesting too to recognise the significance of some discords which we let go by, smudged over by that bright mist, that took us many years and caused us much unhappiness before we resolved them.

The sex part, it goes without saying, was among the most important. We were on a glorious high the whole time. This side and that of forty, we were like a couple of young honeymooners, just into or out of bed, walking with hands gripped wherever we went, sitting with bodies touching, urgency flaring from a mere kiss of greeting any time – even at midday with lunch on the table and the baker at the back door. We didn't have to read any books telling us how to accomplish 'The Joys of Sex' – could have written a beauty ourselves. I used to feel that I was able to give my whole self and my whole love, just hand it all over, and know I was safe. It was one kind of freedom, the release of all the passion in my nature – the 'fire in my belly'. Whatever the years have brought me, whatever the gifts of the gods that didn't come my way, that's one that did, and it belongs to me and who I am for ever.

    I have to bring myself down out of those blissful clouds of memory, and digress a little. By this time I was thirty-eight, but thought I could still manage to have a baby, and Oh! how dearly I wanted one! You just said, 'If it comes, all right, but if it doesn't well, we're a bit old for it, aren't we?' So the sex department was free of any contraceptive impedimenta, and Oh you young females on the Pill, you can't imagine the distasteful and distressful tricks we had to go on with before that catalytic discovery – the jellies, pessaries, caps, douches, devices we had choice of – though of these I had been free for I forget how many years. I had known a man who was an osteopath, and he had a fabulous theory about contraception. The young females of the Trobriand Islands, he said, were accustomed to free love all their adolescent lives, but it was a great mystery that they never conceived until they were married and wanted to. The osteopath said he knew the secret, which he was kind enough to tell me (he didn't tell me how he found it out). As soon as the act of love is over, the damsel stands up and performs a downward massage of her tummy with her thumbs in a particular way, which keeps the mouth of the womb open and so prevents the sperm from settling itself in. This method I had used when occasion arose, gratefully, but now when I wanted to get pregnant I didn't, so I have never known for sure whether it was efficacious or not, and couldn't have the confidence to recommend it to those in need. Bad luck, that was.

We started to build our life, to make our tapestry, with beautiful rich colours weaving in; the happy times we shared, the fun, the beauty, the friendships, our families – 'Remember the laughter, the music, the wine?' – in our case the home brew. At the same time, though we didn't know it then, our own separate tapestries were weaving themselves.

If we sat down to it together, the memories would come tumbling, and the happy ones would be the same for us both. What of the bicycles? Went everywhere on our bikes, we did, the three of us, as soon as Jo and I learned to ride (as indeed did most of the population, and for all I know does so still). Looking up along Acacia Avenue at about a quarter to nine, it seemed to me like a great flock of birds skimming close to the earth, all those wheels and all those bodies in a great surge of bright twinkling movement, going to the High School, you among them, and later Jo as well. I used to go shopping on mine, with my basket in front. Never rode a bike before then, but I did well – can you remember the loads I used to bring home on it? Not only the everyday fare. Half a case of oranges in a bag home from the packing shed; six-pound bag of sultanas and raisins home from the Co-op; even two flagons of sherry home from the winery in a pack on my back – how did I even have the nerve? At weekends, you of course to tennis on yours, Jo and I to the swimming pool. Down to the river, the three of us, on the evening of a sweltering day, putting our poor hot bodies all puffed up and swollen with heat, into the soft quiet brown cool water of the Lock, swimming slowly along with a lazy side-stroke, looking up at the grand old river gums and the changing shapes and colours of the thin summer clouds. Our lovely sunset rides, three of us again, along Wattle Road, quiet, smooth, easy in the calm of a late summer evening, and the western sky in a blaze.

Ah – what of the hot nights, the wickedly hot nights? And the big mosquito net made like a double-bed canopy by sister Winsome when she lived once in Charters Towers, and had handed over to me? We'd sling it up between the two clothes lines – no rotary hoist for us – and we'd push and carry out the mattress from our bed onto the thick prickly lawn, and there we'd sleep. I remember inspired athletic connubial activities out there, and having a giggle because of a notion that we might have been performing in a circus cage under that great net. We'd wake in the bright hot morning when for some reason the perfume from the chook yard would permeate the air, and get with pushing and shoving the mattress back inside; or maybe the cool change and some rain would arrive in the night, and we'd have to move fast.

Lots of lovely glowing colours are woven into our tapestry by the good friends we made in those days. In the very beginning there was the wonderful luck of Helen and Stuart. They were new to Mildura too, but they'd known you for many years via a tennis club in Melbourne, and Helen was jumping for joy that the club's most eligible bachelor had been nabbed at last, and that he and his wife were coming to live next door.

HELEN

My friendships over the years had been sporadic. My dear, warm, close friends from University days hadn't been much in evidence; scattered when those days were over, some to work, some to marry, some to remote places, our lives went widdershins. Over the Blokes-and-Bosses period, I mostly happened to make a friend from the girls who worked where I did, moving out of the friendship with the job. In my first marriage/pregnancy/wartime period, I was so lonely I'd keep even the grocer's delivery boy in futile conversation as long as I could. I was too poor and too pregnant to be going on visits around Sydney in buses and trams. And oddly, I was ashamed of being poor, I wonder why? I wasn't ashamed of the condition of poverty, but there was something shaming in having only one maternity smock, in putting on potato pie and junket for dinner – not being on equal footing with my peers, I suppose it was. I did have Kate, indefatigable, and I don't think she ever knew how grateful I was to her. Every Thursday evening she would come, and we'd talk about music, life, art, literature and love, and bless her for ever, though we've lost touch now these many years. In the interregnum between one spouse and another, I was too busy with my own life and my daughter to get into friendships with women. But now! A woman for friend, just over the fence, to share lives with, good times and bad, to give me pointers on how to fit myself into the pattern of life that was now to be mine, that of the domestic lady in the country, the wife, mother and citizen act after seven years of Blokes-and-Bosses.

One of her first jobs was to teach me to play Solo, a regular Saturday night affair. A Mildura amenity was the 'porker', an extra-large bottle holding draught beer which needed drinking before a weekend was out. The porker and Solo are entangled in my memory, and one of those bottles remains in my kitchen cupboard yet, the only rolling pin I've owned in over thirty years. In spite of the times I've looked back on, when I cooked for the family in Mosman and the school in Baulkham Hills, I was no 'afternoon-tea' cook, and would sit aghast at the variety of dainty cakes and cookies presented to my mazed city eyes, let alone the toppling sponges and – truly I'd never heard of pavlova before then (not as a cake anyway!). Helen was a wizard at all this, and used to roar with laughter at my incompetence, but she never succeeded in passing any ability over. Ten years I lived in Mildura and I was still known at the end of that time as the person who'd bring a 'boiled fruit' to cake-fest occasions. But I had a light hand with the pastry, and that porker rolled out many a fine apricot pie and jam tart.

More than the porker I have in possession to remember her by. The old wind-up gramophone and the box of records came with me whithersoever I went. Once I received a magnificent present of five pounds from somewhere, so I bought some new music, the *Fifth Brandenburg Concerto* and Handel's *Love in Bath* suite. This latter became our party specialty. At a certain stage of the evening and its home-brewed inebriation we'd have our own wonderful dance with this gay and gorgeous music. I can never hear it now without thinking of her (It wasn't till I went to work, after five years' domesticity, that I saved up and bought a radiogram equipped for wonderful, wonderful long-playing records – a whole symphony on one side!).

Dear Helen. We grew veges, we bottled apricots and peaches, we made marmalade and fig jam, we pickled olives, we made home-brew; we went to concerts and the Little Theatre plays with our husbands, three tickets for four people, taking it in turns to baby-sit. When Jo was sick once or twice, she'd take her in to sleep at their place the better to be able to nurse her. Either of us in bother or trouble, the other was there to back-stop. When we went on holidays, she'd keep the garden watered and come in and clean the house against our return; and we'd do the same for her. Dear Helen. She Oh so certainly made a contribution to the happiness with which I was abounding in those glowing days.

LETTER TO MY LOVE contd

At first, though, apart from Helen and Stuart, I was constrained to rely on your bringing home people from school, from tennis, from the Little Theatre. To meet friend material I used to think that a lady coming strange to a country town needed to go to work, play sport, or go to church, and I didn't do any of these for the first five years. But you brought me home good people to love.

 Our families added to the depth and detail of the pattern, inextricably woven in – part of the main warp. You couldn't count as many members as I could, but we saw more of yours, in Melbourne, as mine were mostly in Sydney. But we had great times staying with Nan in the Christmas holidays, in her school at the top of the hill in Vaucluse, which became a kind of family headquarters and central clearing ground for our lot, as Mother was living there. Our mums never met, come to think, and our sisters for the first time when Bette, who used to live in the guest house run by Rose and Perc., mentioned earlier, married your handsome nephew, also mentioned before. Which is its own story.

What of my, who now became our, daughter? You loved her, enjoyed her, had fun from her being with us, and were proud of her good looks and grey matter, but it's no use pretending that it was roses, roses all the way. You said you would leave her handling all up to me, and you did, in the big things, but of course in day-by-day life you had your standards and your preconceived ideas of what a child should do and be. We were happy most of the time, and the only rows we had in those days were over her. I thought you were too hard on her, you thought I was too soft. (I must ask her some time what she thought!) I suppose I was trying to make up to her for the rather ragged times I'd put her through in the unsettled years, and wanted her to feel loved and secure; and you wanted a child who did all the right things, and none of the wrong ones. And Oh! you did find it hard to bear, to see her sitting in the big armchair in the corner, reading, reading, reading, when she 'should have been out playing sport with a bunch of kids.' Lucky for her she wasn't a boy! But this was only in the first little while, until she found her own Helen and had a 'best friend' and her life got a move on.

So went on our life for about five years, full of fun and people, music, books, gardening – Oh for your broccoli and cauliflowers! and for my stocks and sweet peas! – you with your tennis and the ballyhoo of tournaments, I swimming and sunbaking, often sowing, making clothes for Jo and myself; Jo growing up and going to High School, bringing her friends home. A lovely memory is sitting by the beautiful great mallee-root fires you used to build, all of us reading or listening to music, quiet, content, sometimes chuckling, sharing – will I ever forget the laughter when Jo was going through *Babbit*! Our first LP record was the

Tchaikovsky Violin Concerto, which lasted us for about six months. Two new records a year we used to have, one for my birthday in December and one for yours in May, my present to you being what young Helen would have called 'a busman's present', as I always chose one that I wanted. We had the ABC concerts on the radio – I recall Menuhin playing a Beethoven violin piece, like an angel out of heaven, and us weeping with its beauty. The music we bought then – the Dvorak Cello Concerto, the Schubert A Major Quartet with two cellos, the Tchaikovsky Trio – to hear any of these now takes me bang straight back to that little room in Mildura, and my feeling of being 'still at the centre'. Do you remember when Jo brought Ferry home for friend, how she'd kneel on the floor with her head on a cushion, bum in the air? That was how she could shut out the world and really listen. At the end of our parties, too, people all happily full of home brew departing at about 1 am, and you – 'Just stay for half an hour or so and we'll play you something marvellous', and the slow movement of the Cello Quintet would resound through Duke Street in the quiet night. Remember the time when you got very cross with the Whosits over the way playing their new radio flat out, and you going across to ask them to turn it down a bit? How glad they were to have their own say about neighbour's music; and you had to beat a retreat.

It was a lovely, happy time, the tapestry growing and glowing rich and good. Then it went a little thin for me. Many of our good friends had left Mildura; there was no little child; I wished for something more to give my life to. Well might it be said that I somewhat overprayed myself!

THE MENTALLY RETARDED CHILDREN

There was a notice in the local paper, a public meeting being called with the object of establishing a Day Centre for Mentally Retarded Children, to be addressed by some very big wigs – our local MP, the Minister for Health, the Director of Mental Health Services. A committee was formed to get it on the move, with Barbara somehow a member of it. How to make a start? First get your premises? First get your Supervisor? (There was a known small number of children who would benefit.) Oh, how it niggled me! Something worth doing. I came out of a committee meeting on a hot, still evening, talking to one Thea Fleming who had been nominated Secretary – a trained Special School Teacher, then Primary teaching. Says I, 'Which way are you going?', and we walked up Acacia Avenue together, pushing our bikes, talking it over. Says I, 'I suppose they'd have to have a really trained person to take on that job – I'd love to have a go at it, but I suppose it would be terribly hard,' and Thea says 'No, it isn't terribly hard, and the kids are good fun. You could do it,' she says, 'I'd help you.'

So I stuck out my big neck, went to see the local MP and offered myself as Supervisor, and there I started the most vital, extending and rewarding years of my life. It began in the weeks before we opened the Centre, the working-bees by good-hearted tradesmen to get the old Community Centre hall into suitable shape, myself seeing parents and helpers, trying to get hold of equipment and work out a program. I was busier than I'd been for a long time, and of course both scared and excited at what I'd let myself in for.

I used to have a time in my everyday week for working things out – if I had a problem I'd say to myself, 'I'll leave that till Tuesday when I'm doing the ironing.' On one such day I suddenly downed iron, pushed pile of garments away, put my head down on the table, and let my cry out. I cried for all the kids everywhere who needed Centres like ours, and I cried for their mums and dads and families. A very useful and valuable cry, that one. When something might happen that got under my guard, I'd push the feeling of tears away and say to myself, 'I've had my cry for you,' and then I could get on with it.

And Thea was right. Though we had lots of hard work, we had lots of fun and lots of love too, myself and the voluntary helpers. The children were so happy to be in a 'school' where everything was planned for them and their needs, where those who had been in Primary schools weren't picked on or laughed at, and where those who had been kept at home and tucked away out of sight now had company and friends. The basic fun and affection in their natures was free to come out, and we never ceased our amazement at the care they showed for each other, especially for anyone who seemed to be more in need than they themselves.

These Centres were only in their infancy in those days, sprouting all over Victoria. There was no course of training for Supervisors, and those who were in charge (totally untrained, like me, or with some Primary or Kindergarten skill) were operating rather on the trial and error method, learning as we went. We got help from each other, in seminars, and from people in the Mental Health Department. We needed all we could get!

I was lucky I had Thea. She was as good as her word, and I couldn't have done without her.

The poor lady didn't have much notion of being a Secretary, and after the monthly committee meeting she'd come up to see me on the next Saturday afternoon, carrying her Minutes and papers in her satchel, which also bulged with a bottle of beer.

'How will I write this letter … What will I say to these people?' she'd ask, and I'd fix up the correspondence for her while we knocked off her bottle. Then I'd get mine out of the fridge, and say 'How would you go about …? What can I do with …? and she'd fix up my difficulties with the children. No wonder we started an enduring friendship.

One thing I thought up for myself, and I still take joy in the memory. On Wednesday mornings we used to take everyone – well, you could say swimming. We moved from the Community Centre hall after a couple of years, and had the use of an old house, which had many advantages, one of which was the gate in the back fence – it opened onto the grounds of the Olympic pool. We'd change all the kids at our Centre and then traipse through the gate, someone pushing big Beryl in her wheel chair, everyone with excited, shining faces. Not one of them had ever been taken to the pool before. The caretaker was very good, and would come across to help, but we never had any cause to fear danger, the kids were too timid to go deeper than waist high in the shallow end, and then mostly hanging on like mad to me or one of the helpers. But never could I forget how they loved it. Trevor, for instance, a boy of twenty, severely spastic but able to walk. When I tried getting him to hold onto the side and kick, he brought his legs up in front of his body to do it – in the foetal position I suppose. 'Okay feller,' I thought, 'I'll fix you,' so I'd turn him on his back, hold him by the shoulders and tow him across the width of the pool, myself going backwards of course, with him kicking away ecstatically and calling out his one word, 'Boom-yer! Boom-yer! Boom-yer!' And I can still see Beryl, who had no power in her legs at all, but she used to manage locomotion, when not in the wheel chair, by shoving herself along somehow on her bottom. She was about twenty-five, and a fat creature. The first day we took her swimming! She got herself fair to the middle of the bub's pool, and sat there splashing in delight, crying out, 'Look at me! Look at me!'

I used to take them all on excursions out into the town whenever there was any public occasion, Floral Festival and such, partly for their own enjoyment, and partly so the townspeople would get used to seeing these kids and get over their initial reaction, which was fear.

For five years I did that job; we began with six children on three mornings a week, two voluntary helpers coming each day – eternal thanks to the noble souls. When I left we had nineteen children on five mornings and two afternoons, and a salaried assistant. Then Whit moved from Mildura and that phase was over.

Let me jump twenty years to the time in 1979 when we went to Mildura for the 25th anniversary of the opening of the Centre. The phrase 'Great oaks from little acorns grow' kept running in my head. There were sixty-five children then and a staff of over thirty, with trained specialist teachers, bus drivers, cleaners, gardeners. The joy it was, pure joy, to see the modern spacious building, the special rooms for pottery, painting, craft, games; to see the beautiful work being done, to see the children learning skills we would have thought impossible, to hear of imaginative activities which are involving the children with other young people in the community. That was one thing that transported me. The other was to meet again the seven or so children who had been there with me, now of course adults in their thirties and forties, even fifties – how their faces lit up when they saw me, and Whit too – the delight in the great beaming smiles, the kisses and the handshakes. This after twenty years. No chance of their ever forgetting anyone who cherished them. No chance of my forgetting that day as long as I may live.

LETTER TO MY LOVE contd.

That happy ten years – that wonderful time – all those warps and wefts in our harmonious tapestry – what of the threads and colours that clashed?

Not only were we normal and had to disagree some of the time, but you were forty-four and I thirty-eight when we started life together, and we had very well-formed minds and manners of our own. As we are both now in our seventies, the clashes have mostly been relegated to limbo in the general aim of our living it out in peace and concord; but there are two or three I wish we had resolved then, and saved the sorry time that came later.

One clash, very early on, was to do with Jo's having her shower in the mornings. You had lived with your sister Bess and her family for some long time, and every single morning Bess used to yell at young Margot, 'Get out of that shower!' I wondered if you thought that yell was part of all domestic life? I could never understand your producing it – Jo wasn't there so very long or keeping anyone else out of the bathroom, or running us out of hot water. Why in the name of heaven didn't we nominate, say fifteen minutes, and that would have been that and the end of it? – Because you were too angry. A silly little thing to remember? But that kind of anger seems to me to put the angry one out of action, to knock out the chances of any reasonable discourse.

Not that I never get angry. But in my family, there were two emotions that never got a person anywhere at all. If I expressed being sorry for myself over a pain in my spirit, I would have received a scornful response from my brothers, of 'Diddums wassums itsy bitsy bubba,' and, as with a pain in my body, I'd have to take it away into a corner by myself until I got over it. It was much the same with being angry, except perhaps the 'Diddums' would have been said with mocking laughter. We had the example of one of our sisters who had the very devil of a temper, poor soul. It would flare to the firmament over any old something/nothing, and she a lunatic in its blaze, even unto grabbing the nearest whatever to swipe one with. Then it would fizzle out and be quenched in floods of tears down one's neck, with hugs and kisses and 'I'm sorrys'. It didn't make much sense or achieve anything, and it was all to do again next time.

(When I went to New Zealand in 1938 I stayed for some weeks with this sister, Mary, ten years older than I, and never close to me in the family. So glad to see me she was, so kind and loving to me, she made me anxious to get myself into a bed-sitter of my own before she spoilt the cordialities by one of her terrible tempers. Which I did. Years later she told me she was longing with all her heart for me to stay on with them. For a woman married at thirty-seven, pregnant at thirty-eight, stranger in a strange land, fitting herself to domesticity (without much money) after more than twenty years of 'going to work', it would have been good to have a sister around. I never owned up to why I'd gone.)

So much for anger. I think it's a pity we didn't try to sort it out from the start, and for many years it was as though you felt your anger was a weapon to frighten and bring anyone to heel; whereas I always felt mine was stuff to be ashamed of.

There was another clash, one that we laughed at then, and only much later did we find out that it was no laughing matter at all, at all, and bitterness came into it. Our Friday night argument, always the same one so help me. Friday was your night with the boys in the Club or pub (I've never known why they become 'boys' as they go in the door), and coming home at whatever time in whatever state of insobriety. This I had no cause to mind about, and I didn't. It was often good fun if you came in with Fordie. I'd just push the pots with the dinner in them to the back of the good old fire stove and be prepared for a bit of a session, with a few bottles to be opened, the biscuits and cheese to be brought out, and of course the dish of home-pickled olives. Then there'd be the sport of the blokes firing the olive pips, perhaps at a fly that might be walking around the edge of the light shade. But I don't remember how our argument would start, after the 'boys' had gone and dinner was dispatched. Woman's work and woman's place it was. The man provides the food, clothing and shelter, and it's a woman's job to look after him, the home and the family; and off we'd go.

'It isn't every woman on earth who rejoices in being a slave to a man, a house and a bunch of kids.'

'She isn't a normal woman if she doesn't.'

'Whatever kind of person she is? Whatever her abilities in other directions?'

'A proper feminine woman should accept her place and her job and be happy doing it.'

'If she's got any brains of course she can do it, but don't expect her to like it.'

'If she doesn't like it then she shouldn't get married.'

On and on with variations of this theme, till in the end I'd laugh and give over, not really believe you were serious, not dreaming of the strife that was storing up.

LITTLE LETTER TO MY BODY

By now you were coming up fifty. In the last year in Mildura, you, my good strong healthy body, took the first steps on your downhill track, with intimations of your menopause. There were erratic periods, and fearful dreams, waking as well as sleeping, of becoming nothingness after death, not so much 'rolled round in Earth's diurnal course, with rocks and stones and trees,' as rolling round for ever and ever in the infinity of space. Also I was having the first tentative attacks by the enemy, insomnia, which was to become a very familiar foe. I would lie awake in bed, Whit a log in the arms of Morpheus beside me, and my arm reaching for some water and (truly) an Aspro; and then, daring, for a cigarette, hoping he wouldn't wake and be cross.

Whit and I both remember Ron, a postman who lived at the end of our street, in spare time a wonderful masseur and manipulator, whose steel fingers used to fix the wrenches and sprains of the footballers. To Ron I took your back, now beginning to complain, I do verily believe, from the time I fell out of a big pear tree when I was eleven. A good man, Ron, but – well his own cheerful words when you turned pale green one time and started to crumple, 'Urts, don't it?' He certainly helped, and I wish he lived at the end of our present street, indeed I do.

Ron was one. To the eye doctor another, when the figures in the telephone book got too blurry to read, and so to your first pair of reading glasses. And to the dentist I took your remaining well-filled teeth and your partial dentures. A young fellow he was, I don't think he'd ever seen such a mouthful of mended old battlers. What best to do? Reef them all out and be done with it? Better get the senior expert to have a look. 'Patch 'em up,' says he, 'Patch 'em up.' So t'was done. One old warrior was there at the back, just about all amalgam, that was the anchor for the bottom denture. 'Old Rowley,' I called it, after the crazy old race horse that won the Melbourne Cup back in 1930 something, and doped, so they said, to the eyes. It got some more patches and lasted you quite a few more years. Even so, body of mine, you were good to me and I was lucky to have you.

Whit's mother used to come up and stay with us for a month or so in the winter. Bless her. She hated the idea of traveling all night in the train, in a sleeper; A, she might have been murdered in her bunk, and B, her modesty couldn't abide the idea of undressing in the same cabin as someone else, a stranger. She was terrified of aircraft traveling, because she might be sick and have to ask the hostess for a bag, and her modesty couldn't abide that idea either. But these things she did, trying to find the one she hated least. At first she was a bit frightened of me because she thought I was 'clever', but that was forgotten once I got her laughing.

LETTER TO NANA ROSIE

You were the greatest lady in the whole wide world for being clean and tidy. If I went out and let you loose with the brooms and dusters, the place would be gleaming and spotless when I got back, and so tidy! Every house has to have at least one place where people dob things. Mine was a shelf on the kitchen sideboard, but you had to have that tidy too. For weeks and weeks after you went home I'd find collections all put neatly into little bowls or pots – two bobby pins, a razor blade, three trouser buttons, two bits of chalk, a pencil stub and a packet of cigarette papers with one left. 'I didn't like to take the responsibility of throwing anything out', you'd say. Later on when I went to work, when I'd leave in the morning and say I hoped you'd find plenty to do, there'd be a gleam in your eye and I'd know you had a plot. When I'd discover that you'd tidied the kitchen drawers, you'd be gratified and say, 'You do notice things don't you Barbara?' I just could not get you to believe that they hadn't been tidied since your last visit of a year before, true as it was. Of course I noticed! You thought I was a hopeless housekeeper, bless your sweet tidy heart and soul. It was all the life you'd ever known, keeping house for your husband, two daughters, and this one marvellous son (my spouse). I'll swear the look in your eyes when he came in the door was saying, 'How did ever simple little me produce anything so wonderful.' But the tidiness habit never rubbed off onto him, not one skerrick of it, then or ever. 'I'm sure it isn't my fault,' you'd say, 'if he's so untidy. I was always telling him to pick up his clothes.' 'Yes Nana,' I'd answer, 'your voice would be telling him while your body was bent over doing it for him.'

Dearly indeed as I loved you, Nana Rosie, you put a rod in pickle for whomever your daughter-in-law may have been, but specially for the one you finally got, one brought up in a big family where one of the commandments was 'Thou shalt not leave anything about for someone else to tidy up.' I still can't believe my eyes, after all these years, when they fall on things, things, things just left where they've been finished with. And not only you, Nana, pickled that rod, but your daughter Bess too, with whom both you and Whit lived for many years. So he would leave a thing down somewhere, and one of you would pick it up and put it away, and, specially going off to work in the morning, when he'd start to query, 'Where's my …' On the instant there'd be two women on their feet to fetch and carry. I set my face against this sort of behaviour from the start, and when breakfast would be over and Himself on his feet, I'd grab the paper and put my nose in, so come the 'Where's my …' I'd mumble 'I don't know, dear.' He must have wanted to strangle me, often. Said to me once, 'The trouble with you is, you're so used to getting yourself off to work in the mornings you think everyone else can do it,' and what I thought was joking was in dead earnest.

I couldn't stop your housewifely activity, you couldn't stop yourself. It was all there was to do. Housework all done, I'd find you digging up weeds in the garden. How well I remember you on Mondays, washing day, and I used to boil up the copper (so long ago it was). The thing to do, washing finished, was to take a bucket of the hot soapy water and scrub the kitchen floor. I had to watch you like a hawk or you'd have the bucket and be down on your knees. 'Stop that, Nana!' I'd say. 'I can do it, Barbara.' (proud you, and nearly eighty years old). 'I know you can dear, but you shouldn't be doing it when I'm here.' Then, cunningly, I'd think to get you on your most sensitive spot. 'What would the neighbours think,' I'd say, 'if they came in and saw your hale-and-hearty daughter-in-law standing here and letting her old Nana scrub the floor?' Your answer would be, 'They'd just think what a nice old lady she must be.'

The time you decided to go home by plane! So brave! You were afraid of August, the windy, stormy month and sure enough, the day you were booked to leave an icy gale was blowing. No way would you put off your departure, you stuck out your little chin and got yourself aboard the dear old DC4. Braver than brave, you had two bottles of your Whit's home-brew in a separate bag, to take and show the Melbourne lot what beautiful beer he could make; and you were terrified it would blow up in the plane. What a torrid hour you must have had! You told us after, you sat rigidly still not game to move or have even a drink of water, let alone a cup of tea, for fear to be sick and have to bother the hostess; and the beer like a bomb at your feet. Collected at the airport, your control gave way, and you were sick all the way home in the car. But victory, victory, the beer stayed safe.

I love the way you were still vain of your appearance up to the last time you stayed with us; you were eighty-three, and it was about six months before you died. You were always dainty and always in a 'good' coat, 'good' hat and 'good' shoes, though no one knew how you afforded them. Darling Nana, I especially love to remember making a dress for you. Choosing the material and the pattern was an afternoon's business, and the fittings were fun. The sleeves had to come just below the elbow to hide the scrawnyish top part of your arms, but be short enough to show your neat wrist. You liked a collar to hide the wrinkles in your neck, but the V in the front could be just a little bit lower than the pattern said because that part of you was smooth and nice. The length of the skirt was a momentous matter; you liked to show the well-turned leg and neat ankle you were proud of, but we had to be in the fashion and just exactly so. I'd be fitting say the sleeve, and should I say 'Is that right?' there'd be just something in your voice when you said 'Very nice,' that would tell me it wasn't. 'Would you like it half an inch longer?' I'd ask, and Oh so gently you'd say, 'If it isn't too much trouble.' You knew precisely what you wanted, and had a delicious mixture of diffidence in asking me for it, and determination to have it. I know we were both so pleased and proud with the result that we accomplished another dress next visit, so you had one summer one and one winter one, both blue, and I think they 'saw you out'.

You died as you would have wished to, being the minimum of trouble to anyone. Took ill one Tuesday and left us the next Sunday, so we were prepared for your going, but there was no lengthy dependence and looking-after. And your departing words, to your beloved son at your bedside, were, 'I don't think I've made many enemies.'

TO MY MOTHER

I wonder how many dozens of letters we wrote to one another, in that eight years after I went to Mildura and before you died? I kept you informed about our doings, the small matters of daily life – I had made a new dress for Jo – I had preserved twelve bottles of apricots and six of peaches – the grapefruit marmalade had jelled perfectly – the sweet peas were all in bud – Whit was a great success in his part in *Arsenic and Old Lace* ... When I was working with mentally retarded children my letters were chock full of plenty to tell. You kept me in touch with the doings of the school, *Edgeworth*, where you now lived and worked with Nan, and you passed on news of the family – who was marrying, having a baby, traveling, had been ill and now was well. Wonderful letters, full of your own personality and with your own individual quirks of style. I wonder if anyone will ever read our correspondence. You had a penchant for keeping letters from your near and dear, and after you died Nan donated piles of them, along with diaries, photo albums, old family records, heaven knows what-all, to the Mitchell Library, where they now reside, and my letters to you among them, filed under the 'Hall Papers'. I rather incline to keep letters myself, some letters, the rich and lively ones, and Nan has a bundle of yours to me over the Mildura time which are to end up in the Mitchell as well. I hope someone or other gets some fun out of them some day.

Often we got ourselves to Sydney in the long school holidays, and I recall especially January 1951 when we all congregated joyfully for the great occasions of the first two grandchild weddings, Hilary to David early in the month, Wendy to Andy towards the end. Hilary and David's was at St. Thomas's, Rose Bay, and the reception was at *Edgeworth* itself.

It was a joyous day for you. You loved the idea of the wedding party being held at home, as your own had been, and there was the added delight that Hilary wore your very own wedding gown, preserved for over fifty years – a gown indeed, so much more than a frock or a dress, created from rich flowing satin with a tight waist and leg o'mutton sleeves. It was a high heyday in the family, we were all flourishing and our lives humming along cheerfully; troubles which were to come hadn't yet poked up their nasty little heads, except for Pev, always in and out of hospital since he came home from the war in 1919 with one leg off; but he was well that day. We were all there, with spouses and families, except for George who made it to the second wedding. Bob came from New Guinea, Barbara from Mildura and Mary from New Zealand (announcing excitedly that she was going to 'eat too much, drink too much, and talk too much') and there were grandchildren all over the place. You were seventy-eight, energetic in mind though your body was slowing down. (Here I remember your poor old feet. The bones of your toes had receded somehow back into the balls of your feet, and the toes were all flabby and curled over. One of my particular jobs when I was in Sydney was to bathe and massage those painful feet. And, since nearly forever, of course to do your hair).

The day of the wedding the house was brimming with your children and grandchildren all dressed or dressing in their nice new clothes, and Lesley, at last satisfied that she looked her part as mother of the bride went into your room to see if you needed any help. You dismissed her serenely, saying 'Barbara is coming in to help me dress.' Which I did, and then sat you down for me to do the hair and put on the hat; and just a tiny bit of make-up to put on the face (so deep the wrinkles). Some face cream patted in, then just a little of liquid make-up over, and a brush of powder –

all my cosmetics, you never made up your face in your whole life. Then, very tentative, you asked what did I think of just a touch of lipstick? But not if I thought you'd look like a raddled old woman. The final drop in your cup of happiness that day was when the bride, instead of throwing her bouquet to the assemblage as she was leaving, gave it to you, beloved grandmother.

Rejoicings were all to do again a few weeks later for Wendy and Andy, and we could all wear the same new outfits as before. The old wedding gown was worn once more, not then but six years later by granddaughter Esta; but after that I think it fell to pieces.

There was another occasion for the family assembling, this time all except the ones over the water. It was in 1955, when Nan called us to a family conference to help sort out a problem Time had presented to her. You had helped Nan with her school for fourteen years, in charge of the kitchen and the commissariat, and as grandmother extraordinary to the dozen or so boarders. Now, at eighty-three, you wanted to 'retire'. You had your own self-contained flat adjoining the school, and Nan had engaged a fine woman to come for the job, but the trouble was, could you keep out of the kitchen? You belonged to the generation to whom waste of food was a sin of the worst kind. For so long, all your own married life for a start, and then with the school, economy over food – making the little bits spin out and go round – was a way of life, a religion, and you certainly had a genius for it. I'm prepared to swear you never bought, actually paid money over, for bones to make soup, but great delicious potfulls of it you could magically turn out. It was many years before I could exorcise your ghost when I was buying two-bobs-worth of soup bones, and to this very day you haunt me every summer when my wretched plum tree gets thick with unwanted plums and I let them drop on the ground and don't make any jam, sauce or pickles. To get you to promise to keep out of the kitchen and let Mrs Lewis perpetrate whatever sins of throwing out she might get up to, or whatever extravagances of buying for instance bacon instead of 'begging' pieces from the grocer – that was the job of the family conference. At last it was achieved by your being persuaded to go to Les in Wagga for a time while Mrs Lewis got herself into operation.

How gallant you were, sitting there while your children talked you over, making decisions about you; uneasy, yet proud of your brood. When the day was over and all were gone off except Nan and myself, I went in to kiss you goodnight, and I was flooded with a feeling of kinship, sympathy, grief, admiration – just awareness of you, your life and your spirit. You held me in your arms and I just let it all go in weeping. I didn't say why, I couldn't have, but I think you knew.

Three more years you lived, in your little flat, with your books, radio, pens and paper, and with the school children just through the door, still able to come to you for a pat and a boiled lolly when things went badly for them. With your own offspring and their offspring ever coming to visit, friends and relations too. Becoming a very old lady, your body wearing out. Your mind, never!

You had a tremendous capacity for life. I think of you thrusting through it like a magnificent figurehead on a great galleon facing whatever waves the elements might conjure. You were always seeking, questing for ideas, reasons, the meaning of life. You had plenty to thrust through, with ten children in seventeen years; a struggle to make the pennies go round when they were young, a struggle to cope with ten lively minds and personalities as they grew up. You had your struggles with your husband too, though he had been dead since I was twenty, and it seemed to us that you had forgotten all his prickly traits and treasured his memory more as each year went by. He was a stern, hard man, who believed in Right and Wrong and no grades or excuses in between; you must have had your fair share of fun getting your kids out of trouble with him, and yourself too, as your faith was all emotion, love, drama and adventure, as against his which was to Do the Right Thing, Respect your Betters, and Have Security.

Nan rang me one Sunday night in 1958 to tell me you were very ill, and somehow or other I managed to get aboard a plane next morning. It meant dozens of telephone calls, as I was in the job of Supervisor of the Mentally Retarded Children's Centre, and I had to ask the Committee for leave of absence; which they gave me, but it meant the Centre had to be closed *pro tem*, and all the mums and helpers had to be notified.

Off I went, with my suitcase and basket, carrying oranges, asparagus and all sorts of Mildura goodies, and found my mum in bed attended by three of my sisters, a day nurse and a night nurse, a doctor coming twice a day, and in an atmosphere of tension, drama and excitement which part of you could even have enjoyed. I hadn't seen you for nearly a year. You looked me over, said you liked the colour of my dress but the style was too young for me, and that I was lucky my hair hadn't gone grey. You enjoyed the sight of the bounteous basket, told me how dear oranges were in Sydney and not nearly as sweet and juicy as the Mildura ones, then I was dismissed. So it was with all of us who came, one by one, from remote parts. Mary came from New Zealand, was looked over, had her gift accepted, then she was asked if she still had her own teeth, told she should have her hair cut and set while she was in Sydney, and when she was dismissed I heard you say, 'She looks well … you can tell she's a person of consequence where she comes from'. You had to satisfy yourself how each one of us was getting on in the world, and how our physical selves were holding out.

You gave the poor nurses the absolute hell of a time. You had been a Christian Scientist for many years, and always been interested in mental healing and the power of the mind over the body, reading all you could get hold of on such subjects. You still simply could not believe that medicine – 'Drugs' as you called it, with a wealth of contempt and scorn in your voice – could do you any good. 'Come on dear, take this,' the poor nurse would say. 'What is it?' you would rasp. 'Just something to make you feel better'. 'I don't want it; I'm not going to take it.' 'Now be a good girl, dear, the doctor says you're to have it.' 'Don't you call me a girl! Little whippersnapper like you ordering me around!' 'It's what the doctor says dear, now come on, drink it up.' 'Ugh – I hate it – insulting my body,' you'd say, and finally swallow it, and for two pins, I'd feel, throw the glass at the girl.

No nurse satisfied you. The week I stayed there we had a constant change over. You couldn't stand young people to nurse you, I suppose because you couldn't believe they could know enough in their short little lives to look after someone as old and wise as you. And the poor woman had not only to contend with you, but with your dancing-attendance daughters too, and an atmosphere highly charged with emotion and anxiety. As a new nurse would step in the door the eyes of the sisters would pierce her clean through, deciding on the spot if she was the right type, and had good, sound common sense. They certainly mistrusted one like poor Sister Harley, who even had the cheek to be attractive as well as young.

As for the time you gave the Church of England minister! Though you hadn't attended this church for forty years or more, you were a religious woman and a great lover of the Bible. Nan thought best to get the local man of God to come and see you, which he did, and used to read the Bible to you. He was a man with a good presence and a good voice, and had reason rather to fancy himself as a reader of the Book, but he cut no ice with you. You had tried to understand, and knew your Bible as well as he knew his, I fancy, and you would stop him in his mellifluous flow and ask him the meaning of a verse, as when he came to 'In my father's house are many mansions.' This was something you had never been able to understand. What did it mean, having many mansions, which are large, in a house, which isn't? So you asked, 'What does it mean, young man?' The minister didn't explain to your satisfaction, but went into a spiel about how God was preparing a very special mansion for you to go to, but 'That's no good to me, young man,' you said. 'I want to go where the everyday, ordinary people go.'

The days and nights of a week went by, and you seemed much the same. So then came the hardest thing I ever had to do. I had to make up my mind, stay or go home to Mildura. Clearly your life was coming to its end. How long? No-one could say. Days? Weeks? There were day and night nurses, the doctor, the minister, four daughters beside me now that Mary had come, family and friends in and out by the umpteen dozen. Mildura was suspended in my absence. I decided to go.

Someone drove me to the airport. In those days one had to walk from the terminal out across the tarmac to the aircraft, and that walk I remember, my head held high, my back straight, and up the steps I went and into the plane. Only when we were aloft did I bend and let myself weep. I knew I would never see you again. It was four weeks later that the next phone call came, summoning me to your funeral.

LETTER TO JO

Meanwhile you grew from nine to nineteen. From Primary, through High School, to University. I wonder what sort of mum I was? Like most mums I suppose, good in spots. I can remember some times when I did well, and others when I didn't. I wonder if your memories are the same? Your life, now you are in your forties, is still going at a gallop, and you wouldn't be stopping in your tracks to look over your shoulder. But I'd like to put some of mine down, and some of the good fun.

I did well enough telling you the facts of life when you were a little kid and wanted to know, reading you the book that horrified Mrs Lees. I promised myself when I started this exercise that I'd never say 'How times have changed', but let what I'm writing say it for me. Here's one example that I'll bet you don't even remember. During the first year we were in Mildura Whit came to me in distress because you told him that 'some of the kids at school had funny ideas about where babies came from,' so you'd taken the book to school and read it to them. He thought this would get you a bad reputation among the teachers! I had prepared you for menstruation so that it was a natural, easy enough affair when it came. I'm not so happy about how I prepared you, or rather didn't, for the onslaught of sex, but more about that later when I get to your leaving home.

We got you a bike for your tenth birthday, and you learnt to ride more quickly than I did – round and round the big peach tree in the back yard one afternoon and you were set for riding to school; and I've already written of the sunset rides along Wattle Road, all of us together. You were lonely at first. Took it out in reading – do you remember going through the *Anne of Green Gables* books at the same time, by courtesy of the excellent lady in the Children's Library who used to keep them aside for you? There was a girl, Marlene I do believe, who lived at the back of our place, a bit older than you, but still, a girl. The big thing for me in your growing up years was how far to stick out for what I believed in, and how far to give in to my knowledge that the worst thing for a kid is to be different from its peers. One thing I was rigid on. Kids 'went to the pictures' on Saturday afternoons in those days, regardless. Any old nonsense or rubbish might be on, and I wouldn't let you go, with Marlene. And Marlene's parents, because of whatever religion theirs was, wouldn't let her go swimming with you on Sundays. Bad luck all round! But it wasn't long before you and Helen found each other, and started a friendship that abides to this day. I used to go down to the old pool with you both, and a few other girls, until you learned to swim and could go off together at weekends.

Music was always a pleasure. There used to be a fine session for school kids' singing on the ABC, and you'd learn a new song every week, which you'd sing around the house, and tootle on the recorder. Lovely old ballads – 'Ho Ro My Nut-Brown Maiden', 'Strawberry Fair' and such. Started begging me for a piano, and at last I saved up the money your dad was still sending for you and bought you one. Never had to badger you to practice, and you were soon playing lovely things.

Still friends with Helen especially, among others, when you went to High School. Used to bring kids in on the way home, and away would go my rock cakes. There were birthday parties. I was against what I thought was nonsense as to the giving of presents, but I had to give in on that – it was part of the proceedings. Hankies, socks, books perhaps, hair ribbons – that reminds me! Plaiting your hair every morning. Two little plaits at first, that grew into beautiful long ones, and in your last year at school a pretty, tossing ponytail.

Was it in your second year that you grew six inches? I had to give all your dresses and uniforms away and start all over again – three big bowls of porridge you'd have every breakfast. And was it the next year that we found out about the flat feet, and for a whole twelve months you had to wear lace-up school shoes all the time, with things called spitzy buttons in them. You were wonderful, never forgot and never complained. Square dancing was the rage, and I can see you, lanky girl (but pretty) in a pink dress, and lumping black shoes on your feet. A milestone dress, that one. Not made by me at home but bought in a shop with my own money saved up when I first started going to work.

Used to go to your Grannie's in Sydney for the holidays – must have been March or September because we mostly went to Nan and Mother in Vaucluse at Christmas. We'd put you on the old

DC4 and off you'd go, poor child, air-sick all the way most like. I can't remember when your dad married Peg, but after that you used to stay with them and Christine, and then John was born. They were happy times, but worse luck they didn't last very long; the marriage went properly on the blink before John was two.

I had the uncomfortable job of giving you this piece of news. It was probably a Tuesday afternoon (my ironing-and-working-things-out time), and when you came in from school I sat you down and told you, and very upset you were. I felt I should try to give you some notion of why, as it seemed to me, from the signs, that it had been the same old story as the first time round. I said, 'I suppose I'd better tell you why my marriage to your dad broke up'. And you said, 'You never have.' (Funny little person, you'd never asked me). So I was for it, to be as fair and honest as I could. I said he and I used to have fights. I told you about jealousy, how it can smite like an attack of illness that a person can hardly help; what a dreadful destructive force it is, and warned you to be on your guard against it. Your dad's blue eyes, his short sight and his flat feet you inherited, but as far as I know, not his monster.

So you went through High School, swopping with Helen for top and second in various subjects all the time. A bright pair – and teacher's bane. No wonder, if you talked at school like you did at home. Helen with us for the weekend and you never stopped. Riding our bikes down to the lock for a swim, I can see you two side by side, tongues going umpteen to the dozen all the way.

Boyfriends were another matter. They took a while to emerge. At first you reckoned it was because no boy would want a girlfriend who was taller than him; then, later, he wouldn't want one who could beat him in Maths; finally you said they were all scared stiff of Whit. But when you got to your last year, somehow there were three boys lined up to take you, Helen and Ferry 'to the pictures' on Saturday nights (I couldn't veto this!), and to walk you home from the school socials, Oh yes, very important. The longest way round was the shortest way home for sure, via all the way down to the milk bar and who knows where else. And what of the excitement next school day, who took so-and-so home, and – the burning question – did he kiss her?

I wrote a piece a few years ago about those days, and here I'll quote from it:

'It was one of the happiest times of my life, I realise, that little six years when the daughter was at High School, and the house was either empty or full of girls. They were so pretty, and funny, and so bubbly! (Wasn't it good – wasn't it <u>good</u> – when it was the fashion for girls to look as pretty as possible, and as much like girls as possible.) How's that for nostalgia! And in summer time they wore full skirts with three/four petticoats underneath, and dainty little blouses; and they wore their hair in lovely flowing pony tails, tied back and showing their sweet young faces, which weren't gauded over either, only trimmed with a little lippy. Oh, weren't they charming!

On Saturday nights when it was our turn for a full house the other two would come to dinner, and there'd be the big business going on in the bedroom as they got themselves dressed up. There was a strict ruling that they must never wear exactly the same clothes twice running, and as they all owned one only 'best' of everything (a skirt, a jumper, a coat, a cardigan, or perhaps a skirt and jacket that even matched, I would be keen to see what changes had been rung, and who was wearing whose blouse to go with whose jacket; and what miracles of variety had been accomplished with scarves and brooches. The doorbell would ring, someone would open the door, and there three swains would be, very shy (and the damsels would be very twittery), and off they'd go, walking would you believe, and with instructions to be home by twelve o'clock.'

You always knew what you wanted when it came to clothes. We had an old Pinnock treadle sewing machine, and I worked wonders with it, making turn-outs to your explicit requisitions. And you likewise, when you got it to yourself. The crazy (for then!) things you'd appear in. At home for the holidays and going to 'the pictures' with us, clad in the very newest clobber, a straight 'shift' and black stockings – every single head turning to stare and tut-tut. And what of those bright red pedal pushers with the black bindings!

One of my good jobs as mum was the terrible, terrible time when your boyfriend, Bob, left you and switched to Ferry. You'd been on a school trip to Broken Hill when it happened, and it was a broken-hearted young lady who came home on Friday night. Gloom descended. Instead of three cheerful chattering girls there was one desolate (and of course silent) one. Ferry was in limbo, and poor Helen in between her two mates didn't know what to do. By afternoon I couldn't stand it, and called you to me for a little talk. First of all we sorted out that it wasn't Bob the boy you were grieving over, it was the loss of face for a start, and then the loss of your two dearest girlfriends. In essence I put it this way: 'Ferry and Helen would be just as unhappy as you. In a confused situation it's always a wonderful help if one person makes up his/her mind. So you make up your mind that you aren't going to lose their friendship. And when you go to school on Monday hold up your head and pretend, if you have to, that you don't care. Don't let the hurt show.'

You sat, as usual, in silence, listening with your whole self. I left you to chew and went into the kitchen. Next thing, I hear you on the phone, very tentative, first to Ferry and then to Helen: 'It's Jo here. I hope we can still be friends …' Next after that, a changed girl came beaming into the kitchen. 'Helen wants me to go to her place for the weekend.' And that was that.

Except for the extra-beaming girl who came home from school on Monday, and 'Guess who asked me to the pictures next Saturday! Geoff Carr!' naming the heart-throb of sixth-form girls. And Geoff was the boyfriend from then on and into first year University.

I don't know why I didn't tell you, and the others (I was the only mum likely to) how sex might smite you. We used to joke and laugh about the traps and pitfalls of the big city (Helen used to say she could hardly wait), but I never sat you down and told you what males were and what they did. I suppose I didn't think I needed to – a girl's private life is her own affair. But years later I was horrified when Ferry told me about the gaps in her knowledge and her weird ideas at that time. I should never have let you lot go off and away uninformed.

It was a long time before I did have that talk with you. You must have been over twenty. My sixth sense told me that 'it' had happened – was happening? So I went into the matter of methods of contraception – it was before the pill, though not long. (How I mourned the bad luck that I couldn't recommend the method of my old friend the osteopath!) You sat as ever in complete silence, and then got up and left the room with this masterpiece of ambiguity: 'Well, I don't need any of them now.' (Were you abstaining, were you pregnant, were you satisfactorily fitted up?)

To go back to the Mildura time. There are lots more bright memories. What of the birthday parties? They went from afternoon to evening do's, at first girls only. Whit and I, and Fordie, would retire to the kitchen and leave you all in the lounge room with the radiogram and about four records; classical was all we had, such as Mozart's *Alla Turca* and Schubert's *Soiree de Vienna*. In no time the flat shoes, stockings and – yes girdles – would be off and stuffed under cushions, and the young ladies 'swift transformed' into a bunch of kids dancing for dear life. I think we only had one, milestone as it was, with boys invited. I even remember the playing of 'spin the bottle', which was as far as any kissing went (at least for all I knew). As for smoking or drinking – not dreamed of for kids still at school, at any rate in sight of a parent or teacher.

More bright people too. Marianne for instance, always the dasher, always first with the latest – hair cuts, smoking, boyfriends, clothes. Her family left Mildura before her last school year, and I can see her yet, when she was up for the holidays, sitting in our kitchen in the first bikini seen in town, having a cup of black coffee and a cigarette for breakfast. Oh Marianne!

And Ferry, mentioned before. Her mum died when she was a kid, and she and I adopted one another, and I became Auntie Barbara. Inspired by helping at our Day Centre sometimes, she took on Special Teaching. She and her husband Peter, and the one-after-another four were a big part of our lives for years. It was a great comfort, for me especially, when you and Garry were in

England, and my grandmother arms were aching for the one and then two granddaughters I hadn't even seen, to be de facto Grandma to that bright lot.

There were some spots where I didn't do so well as a mum, especially when we went through the trauma of deciding what you'd do when you left school. It was a long time before I forgave myself for that. You could have done anything you wanted – but what was it? You didn't know. Whit was set on your taking a teaching studentship – shades of me and my dad! I could have stuck out for you going through university freelance as it were, doing perhaps the Science you were good at, with the help of the scholarship you'd won and most of my salary – but – I didn't have the guts (a personal regret on my own behalf which nagged me for years). So the studentship it was, in Arts. Which has turned out well enough, certainly when you have willing senior kids, but you weren't cut out for handling a roomful of reluctant rampageous juniors.

So you were out of the nest two years before we left Mildura. I hated you being so far away and out from under my wings – which I hope to you were never thumbs. Then we came to Castlemaine, much closer. You were in that funny old flat in Brunswick then, with Helen and the new friend Joy, and we could get to see you often enough.

I'm ending this part of my story with leaving Mildura and starting a different way of life, so I'll end my letter to you as I've done with some of the others. Thank you, daughter, for the fun and friendship you brought into the house.

7. The Course Changes

So we left Mildura and came to Castlemaine – one phase over, another beginning. The first year of it was about the most hellish of my life. Lady Luck seemed gone for ever. All we could find to live in was a horrible little rented house which I hated, though at least it was on a hillside and had a view over sheepy paddocks to the town. I was stricken with the miseries of the menopause – the whole bagful. I was fretting over Jo, not very happy in her first teaching job at Inglewood, and boarding there; also in her first real love affair, and driving her first car.

And shades of my dad! I was teaching, or rather standing in front of classes. I had known I would be in a desolation, feeling lonely and useless after my involvement in the Centre at Mildura, and Whit suggested the High School. He reckoned that as I could handle nineteen mentally retarded kids, ergo I'd easily be able to cope with classes of normal ones. Biggest mistake of his life!

We used to work on the love and affection principle in Mildura. Always I'll remember Michael, waiting for me to arrive, and how he'd clutch me joyfully round the legs as I came up the path. Now I had as many as forty-eight in some forms, boys and girls with the full bounce and exuberance of early teens, but to me, monsters all with horns and tails and an infinity of devilment. I wasn't a teacher's toenail, and I had no business being there in front of them, which they and the Headmaster and I all knew very well. Alas, it was in the days when anyone with arms, legs, voice and a smidgin of learning was welcomed by the Department with open arms, it was so short of bodies; and I was one who imagined that teaching consisted in preparing a lesson and presenting it to a receptive class. I didn't know that I needed a technique for getting the young demons to shut up first. (Love, or at any rate affection, was there somewhere, but not as a top-layer working tool).

My poor husband, in his own battle taking on the responsibilities of Senior Master, would find me crying in the bed beside him when he woke up. My heart used to cringe as I walked through the front door of the school in the mornings. My senses revolted from the smell of school, from the racket in the quadrangle. I didn't know who I was. And I couldn't beg out. No matter how ineffective, I was still valuable as a body, and I was committed.

It got slightly better as the year moved on. I was able to go on half-time, and then the Head suggested that I take on the Library the following year – much more my line. In December I began to feel I was coming back to life, when Lady Luck came beaming and belting out of hiding and found us our beloved house. Made of sandstone, sitting on a hilltop among trees and an old-fashioned garden, we've lived in it for over twenty-five years, and still can hardly believe our luck. We celebrated with a house-warming party a few days after we moved in, all among the packing cases – the idea being that if you wait till you're settled you never have one.

Snug in our little house, with Jo at Sunbury and much happier, Whit and I adjusted to our new jobs, and I found the owners of the horns and tails rather fun after a while. We acquired a little black pup, a very engaging character, and our lives got a move on.

The other day I went down to the building that was the High School for the first six years we were here, and is now the Education Centre. I'd seen a poster advertising 'Dancing For Fun' to be held there on Wednesday mornings, and I thought 'Give it a go, Barbara. You've never had enough dancing in your life, and the young people these days, bless them, take you for who you are. They won't give a damn if someone your age turns up.' It was a fine frosty morning, and there I was clad in woollen pantyhose, warm socks and slacks, two jumpers and a poncho, standing at the foot of the old wooden steps that led up to the hall. They are outside in the open quadrangle – the second storey is only on one side. About a third of the way up there's a small platform, and that's where I saw my first ghost – my husband, twenty-five years ago Senior Master, facing the school assembled in the quad below on Monday mornings. From my place among the staff ranged along one wall I'd look up at him – the husband of my board, bed and bosom. Perhaps I'd still be glowing after some tremendous loving the night before; perhaps smarting from a spat as we'd left for work that morning (or even both at once); often wretched with the visitation of a menstrual period, erratic and copious onslaughts in those days); and certainly in a state of high tension because I'd be going straight to 2A English. And there'd he be, his Senior Master voice saying 'Hands on hearts!' Then leading the school with 'I love my country, I honour the flag, I serve the Queen, and cheerfullyobeymyparentsteachersand the laws.' This over, if there was no music teacher upstairs at the piano to strike a chord, he'd hold out his arm saying 'Take this note ...' and singing 'God ...', and off we'd all go, while he beat the time, with 'God save the Queen'.

On such a frosty morning as it was last week the women staff would be in skirts and twin sets, with silk stockings over blue-purple legs. My feet would be utterly numb with cold, and as they warmed up with the day my chilblains would start going throb, throb, throb. The only alleviation allowable to us was double thickness, but still silk, stockings. The poor girls in the quad didn't even have those. Tunics, lace-up shoes and short socks were what they had, and many and various were the shades of blue and purple in their bare legs.

On this day as I walk up past the platform the ghost disappears, as indeed did the 'Love God and my country' bit and the 'God save' within a few years. But now I bump into the second ghost, myself those years ago, going up to 1D, stumbling and cracking my shin a beauty on the sharp edge of the step above. There was nothing for it but press on to the lesson – sin of sins to leave a class on its own. They were all girls, a lovely bunch of cheerful, chatting kids but, fascinated, they watched in silence for once as the blood welled up. They couldn't contain themselves when it began oozing down my leg and into my shoe. 'Mrs Whitley, your leg's bleeding!' Indeed it was, and I had to give in and send someone for the Senior Mistress. I copped a really splendid ulcer out of that busted shin, though there wasn't any rip in the stocking. So I give a grin at that ghost, and up I go and in the door, to where I once used to stand on the dais and face 1D. And up comes another ghost, or rather a ghost voice. The long hall used to be divided into three classrooms by folding wooden doors, and next to me John Ashdown would be giving a French lesson to 2B, and also to my 1D and also another lot on the other side of him as well. John used to be a Colonel in the British Army and his voice was English, precise, and not so much loud as inescapably penetrating. I could only work on a shuttle system, and do my talking while 2B was writing, and *vice versa*. Dear John. One of our closest friends, and dead these five years. Hail, ghost!

Now I'm inside. The floor is covered with a hairy brown carpet, the folding doors are flat to the walls, and I find the 'Dancing For Fun' lot, like a bunch of parrots. Liz is wearing aqua blue tights, tiny scarlet shorts and a red and white striped T-shirt. Jean has a yellow top, maroon tights, and over them a miniscule black v-shaped – well, thing. I couldn't call it knickers. Heather has a purplish crumpled shirt over blue tights, and Sue a wonderful pair of loose black and white clown's trousers. There's one sombre parrot, Neil, in dark blue top and what I suspect is his wife's black tights. They are all stretching and bending to pop music from a cassette recorder. I discard my shoes and a couple of layers of wool, and I'm flat on the floor stretching and bending too.

Fun it surely is. Next we're improvising, on our own, or taking ideas from one another and from the music, dancing, miming, rollicking, laughing. I'm not too sprightly with the kicking and somewhat creaky with the bending, but I can still dance with my feet and sway my body and arms about. It's a very fine thing to be doing on a cold May morning, and I can't wait till next time. I don't think I'll meet or hear any more ghosts.

UMPTEEN LETTERS IN ONE

For twenty-five years we've lived in Castlemaine. It's been a tightly packed hunk of life, with no high peaks of drama, but an unfolding pattern of seasons and years, a definite progression, a moving on. But. But. In my 'Letter to My Love', about the happy Mildura time, I mentioned the 'clashes and bad patches' that were to come. They came all right. Stories and plays about man and wife conflict are deadly boring to me, and I don't intend to write that kind of stuff myself. But I'll have to go through our 'sorry time' because of the important thing, which is that we got through and over it, to the place where a young friend can say to me, 'You have a tender, peaceful look about you these days, Barbara.' To a truly happy time for both of us, I could say our Indian Summer.

I'd have dozens of letters to write to the people with whom our lives were involved over this time. To my sisters and brothers for instance, as their tapestries grew and developed, with children and grandchildren to colour them, and to deepen the body of mine; to Whit's sisters and their families likewise. How lucky I feel, not only when I think of my old friend Rita with no-one, but as I look about me now, to the richness of the young in my life. I remember the comment of a friend of mine in Sydney one time. After I'd told her of our lovely visits to one niece when we go northwards every year, that I was staying then with another, and that a third was coming that day to pick me up and drive me right across the city and its traffic for a special visit, she said to me 'You seem to be endowed with nieces.' Indeed I am, and nephews too, and I thank them for being, and for being so loving to their ancient aunt (and great-aunt too).

To my darling friends. I've had many of the closest friends of my life in this time, and four of them are now dead. My sister Mary and two of my brothers are dead too. I couldn't thank them enough; I wish I believed we would meet again in the hereafter, and we could carry on our closeness for ever and ever amen.

To my daughter. She has got on with her life, and that's a book on its own. We have the love and fun of a son-in-law and three grandchildren – no more, alas for me and the longed-for babies I didn't have when I married Whit. But we have *de factos*, of course. The girlfriends Jo had at school and university are still with us, and have families. Bless them, and all the young folk we know.

To a host of kids. For fifteen out of the twenty-five years I worked at the High School. A person couldn't do better, if she wanted to belong, to be a real part of a town where she lived. Wherever I go about my affairs nowadays I have greetings and smiles and chats from kids-that-used-to-be. Of course they didn't all like me. I recall a few who simply hated me. That was because I rather hated them – they simply would not return their library books, or simply <u>would</u> talk and giggle in the library. But there was Janet especially. She doesn't know to this day how much I have to thank her for. In the second year, after I'd been such a misfit in the first, I had her in 1D English, and the blessed girl got a crush on me. What that did for the confidence of a lady who thought she was a useless, hopeless, helpless failure in front of a class! It set me up. (We're friends still; she brings her husband and two sons to see us whenever she comes to town).

To Lady Luck. We've had some wonderful holidays. Beach times with good friends, Mary and John; Alice Springs with brother Bob and his wife; to Queensland on Long Service Leave; to our favourite place on the northern NSW coast, where we go every winter. We've made some enduring memories of places and people, and lovely things seen in the good world, creatures and sights of nature we've happened upon (like dolphins shooting the breakers!)

For myself, I've had a couple of trips to England, to see Jo who went away after she was married for a two year 'working holiday' and stayed for ten years. Many times I've flitted off to Sydney to see family and old friends, and to have some joys of the place – the Harbour, concerts, the Opera House, the beaches. Still do this pleasant thing.

To our house. It's chock-a-block with history and charm. It was built with two-foot-thick stone walls, lattice windows, little rooms and passages and doorways. You couldn't call it convenient, but the view is wide from every window, across to the mountain and over to the far-away hills; and we love it very much. It could tell its own story, too, of the many, many friends and family members who have stayed with us at times over these years, and (though it's often been the devil of a squeeze fitting bodies in) the gay, pleasant, happy times it's seen. We are only a couple of hours' drive from the city, therefore handy.

To our garden. The pleasure and the pain. Pleasure in the spring, when it goes on a rampage and there's colour wherever you look. Pain in the summer with the everlasting chore of watering the poor, parched earth, any summer. (I won't mention the utter fag of 'one hour's held in hand' in drought times). We've worked hard at it, both of us, and had our reward; had the joys of 'mucking about in the garden' and watching things grow; and I think we've paid the price too, or maybe stiff backs and legs would have come with the years anyway. Mixed blessing, our garden.

To Lady Luck. I've even done a bit of writing and had a bit of acceptance, my claim to fame being five short stories published and twice a prize (third). And I edited *The Chronicles of Suzy Em*.

To Lady Luck again. Thanks, best of all, for our health. Especially mine, as I've never given up smoking (for longer than four weeks), started in my late teens to solace me in times of stress, and to defy my mother (before we knew the hazards of it). Whit gave it up with much strength of mind some years ago. But anyway, though creaking a bit, we are both fit and well, and no-one believes how old we are.

So. What about it? How did you get here, Barbara? What about that stuff, the 'clashes and bad patches'?

It's simple enough, and an old and very common story.

8. The Winds Drop

LETTER TO ALMOST EVERY WOMAN

I'll tell you what happens. Bloke gets over-occupied and absorbed with his work and its responsibilities. Wife sees their mutuality, their life together, fading into the blue. His interest in sex seems to be going the same way – he's too tired, only wants to close his eyes when he hits the bed. Nothing she can do about it except find a lover, go in for good works or take to the grog, and if she fancies none of them she's got bad luck. Very. When they do get round to it she feels he's not making love any more, the loving has gone, it's just a case of when it's time, it's on, and 'the sooner it's over the sooner to sleep'. For him. She lies beside him, restless and unhappy, remembering their happy hey-day when he used to quote to her from Donne's 'The Ecstasy':

> *So must pure lovers' souls descend*
> *T'affections, and to faculties,*
> *Which sense may reach and apprehend,*
> *Else a great Prince in prison lies.*

What happened to that Prince? she thinks. He's a raggy and tattered fellow now. After a while she gets out of bed, makes a cup of tea or mixes a whisky and milk and sits by the kitchen window looking out at the pattern of trees against the sky. Step two is when she goes back to bed in the spare room. Step three, she sets herself up there as a permanent arrangement. Step four comes later – the sleeping pills.

When they buy a TV set it's worse. It's the kiss of death to those shared evenings with music or books. How she resents its dictatorship! 'Seven-thirty! Sit down, look, listen!' Or eight-thirty or whatever. Of course she joins in the pleasure of a good play, concert or ballet on their occasions, but mostly he's in one room and she in another, each in a separate world. And as for the compulsion of watching sport! How she hates the sound of it, and how he can't ever understand or even believe that she does!

She can see what's happening. She tries to talk to him about it, foolish woman; she hasn't found out yet that it's safer not to put such things into words. They aren't a good way of communication at all, rather of misunderstanding and giving the chance of a cutting comeback soon regretted by the one and never forgotten by the other. She begs him to retire early and chuck the soul-destroying work, and in her desperation says, 'It's reached the stage of the job or me.' She is trying to tell him something, but he takes it as a threat or a 'stand-over' – anathema, that word – and gets his back up properly. He says if she is a proper feminine woman and a good wife she should be understanding and support him. She replies that she doesn't see that it should take two people to live one person's life. The answer to this is that it's her lot and she should accept it.

So she feels he's chosen the job, and she can go scratch. Until then she's never thought of anything but fitting into *his* pattern, which was once *their* pattern. Now she looks within herself for something of her own she has some talent and desire for, looks around at the chances, and goes in for whatever she finds that fits both. In a country town she probably joins the Little Theatre or a craft group. (As for me, I did a correspondence course in Short Story Writing. I was fifty-eight when I finished it, and I won third prize in a small competition with the first story I sent away. I think I paid ten shillings entry fee and won five pounds, and when the story saw the light of day in a little magazine that was roneo'd, to my absolute disgust the ending had been altered and the whole point of the story was spoilt. But – even so!)

Back to my 'Just-about-everybody' couple. By now sex has almost cut out. When he comes to her bedside with a conjugal look in his eye she conjures a bad pain somewhere. She is thinking 'How can I have communion by night when there's been no communication by day?' Idiot woman, utter and total idiot, putting cart before horse. But she feels she is fighting for her very existence as an entity. She doesn't know how he gets on – that's his problem. They are split in two, properly.

So they stumble on, the ties and binds of their twenty-odd years of married life holding them together, famiies, friends, the house, the garden, pets, all the books and music, the daily things they have to do – the whole tapestry. But there's not much life or colour in it (in my case it was rough because Jo was in England and all the company I had with her was by mail. It was also rough because in this period my sister Mary died. My company with her was also by mail; we used to write often, pages and pages, sharing our lives. She had a great sense of humour and a lovely feeling for words (she was a poet), and her letters were something to relish. She was the first one of our family to die, and it was a shatterer).

So there they are, just surviving, and … I was going to write, Bang! Comes his retirement. But the effects of it don't come with a bang, they creep up. She retires as well, thinking they will decide to go somewhere, do something, change the lifestyle – why not? Now's the chance! Also feeling sure he will look for a job to keep him involved in life. But what a catastrophe! He is bereft, severed from all that urgency, commitment, responsibility, everything to which he'd given his life, cut off like a head with a single stroke of the guillotine. And he's too tired out, exhausted, utterly up-buggered to tackle anything else. It's awful. And so boring! Neither has anything to bring home, to contribute. He's lost his identity, except for the continuance of his playing sport – bowls by now – and the 'Aussie' mateship that goes with it. She's lost hers entirely. She isn't living anyone's life, his or hers. Thinks, 'Just as I'm set and ready to spread my wings a bit, he's ready to fold his.' Feels squashed flat. Worst of all, she hasn't any money of her own. It's hard to have an entity if you have no money to spend. What he gives her is what she has, and if she needs any extra she has to ask for it. This is gall and wormwood. (As for me, I stopped writing – hadn't any heart for it, and it was too lonely an occupation – whom do you meet, sitting bashing a typewriter?)

So you get down to the bottom of the barrel. How do you get out? With us it came slowly, bit by bit, only recognisable now when I look back. First we separated, in that I went to England and stayed six months, doing my best to help Jo through a tough time (part of her story, this). After I'd been back a couple of months Whit went to Queensland and worked on his nephew's pineapple farm, and he stayed six months too. By now I felt I couldn't handle my home life with my husband, and I was obsessed with the notion that I wanted a job – something I *could* handle. This was when I was really hit hard by my scatty working career. I didn't have a solid profession behind me to call on. Who'd give a secretarial job to a woman of sixty-one? I thought myself lucky when I had the offer to go back to my job in the school library, at first as a part-time assistant. But it was hard and horrible, school and kids had changed enormously in the two-and-a-half years since I'd left – it was a battle, not the fun it used to be. But it extended me, and also gave me some money. I bought a little second-hand car – wonderful freedom, car of my own!

It was good to find that I wasn't lonely living by myself. I had our dog, dear old chap as he was by then, for protection and company, and there was the obligation of taking him for walks. I'd put him in the Mini and drive out along the back roads, letting him run ahead, then I'd stop and gather fallen sticks from the gum trees for fire kindling. I used to let him sleep in the house, and that made me feel safe and secure. Above all, I found it wonderful to be on my own, in a whole house all to myself. I rolled and reveled in it, practically weeping with the relief of that 'sack of wet sand off my back' (once again!). It had been a grim time. Whit must have been equally relieved to be out of it. I felt I was getting to know myself and what was vital to me, unlumbered, the first time for Oh how many years! It was a heady drop. No doubt I was being a selfish pig, but I think now it had to be.

PABLO

He was an exuberant character of a dog, a kelpie/collie cross, middling size. His coat was long, thick and rather shaggy, black mostly, with a white tip to his fine expressive tail. We got him as a tiny pup, and for thirteen years he gave us a lot of fun. Right from the start Whit set out to train him to be obedient; he used to say 'I can't bear a dog that doesn't do what he's told,' and Pablo got the message very quickly. When people commented on his beautiful behaviour I'd say, 'Well of course, he's a school teacher's dog.'

He was full of go, guts and stingo for all that. He was always clearing off with Rusty, his mate from down the road, we never knew where or what doing, coming home weary and bedraggled, usually at food time. If there was a bitch on heat in even the remote vicinity, there was no guessing when he'd come back; it could be in the middle of one night or the next, covered in mud perhaps, rips and gashes all over him.

If we gave him the command 'Sit. Stay,' he wouldn't move till he was called or whistled. Kids thought this was wonderful, and used to play 'hidings' with him. They'd tell him to stay and then run off and hide, and when they called he'd come and find them.

He was a well-known dog hereabouts, not only where there were bitches. He was a familiar sight going on his walks with Whit, 'over the hills and a great way off', all over the mountain, all along the ridge, by rough old back tracks, through the bush everywhere. I used to reckon even the rabbits knew him, and would start up for the fun of it, getting him into a fury of chasing and frenzy of barking, but never letting themselves be caught.

He was known and marveled at about the town wherever Whit used to go, the tennis club, the pub, even the school. I'd take him with me if I drove up to collect Whit after four o'clock, and I can see him yet, getting pats in the yard from the home-coming kids, or skittering on the gleaming linoleum in the corridor as he ran excitedly looking for his master. Once when he'd been missing for two days and nights Whit spoke to the whole school at morning assembly: 'You all know my dog. He seems to be lost. If any one of you sees him anywhere I'd be grateful if you'd let me know.'

Sure enough, one of the boys reported a black dog. 'Could be yours, sir, been up at our place a couple of days now and won't go home,' and, embarrassed, 'our bitch is on heat.'

During the times we had that dog I used to work at the High School myself, mornings, as Librarian; I was a good one too. I enjoyed working with books and kids, and I simply loved it when someone, eyes shining, would return a book I'd suggested and say 'That was a terrific book! Is there another one like that?'

But part of the job, one year, was a Remedial English class, and my failure with that sticks in my memory yet, not dissolved eight years later. I should never have taken it on. Hopeless before I started. The Head, Tom, a good friend of ours, was very keen to have it, and he talked me into doing it. Six girls, good kids too, but – aged fourteen. It was too late. Words were their dreary dreaded bugbear; words printed in books they could only haltingly follow, a finger traveling across the page from word to word as they went; words written by themselves with painful labour. In Year Nine they were at about Grade Three level. They would be leaving school by the end of the year, when they turned fifteen. Their true minds, bodies, hearts and ambitions had much more exciting concerns than sentences.

I had a set of – Oh perish the woeful memory! – Easy Readers, very short and simplified versions of classics like *Call of the Wild*, *Little Women*, *What Katy Did*, *David Copperfield*. They'd read aloud, by paragraphs, talk about it, and write down summaries of chapters; and maybe it all helped a smidgin, but I doubt it. They were blocked, totally blocked, and they knew it. The poor kids had lived just about all their school lives being behind their classmates, though they liked to present excuses for it.

'I was away sick with hepatitis for nearly a year when I was eight, and I missed out on things the others learnt, and I never caught up.'

'The teacher we had in grade Three hated me. I was frightened of her and I never learnt anything that year.'

'There's no time for reading in our house. Everyone watches telly all the time.'

One of them, Leanne, just shrugged her shoulders. 'I'm just a dumbbell and I know I am so who cares.'

She was surly and hard to get on with, perhaps because she was a little brighter than the others, and more self-conscious.

When I went into the class we were strained, anxious, all of us wishing it didn't have to be. It wasn't much fun for anyone. They resented being hauled out of the camaraderie of their regular class, and being closeted with me in a little room rigged up in half the laundry of the Home Eco. Department, right away at the end of a long corridor. I'd persisted because I'd been handed the job and had to push on with it.

At this time Whit had just retired, and Pablo was getting to be an old dog. He was a bit deaf and would have little 'turns' now and then, but was still full of beans and fathering pups all round town. When Whit went to Queensland to work on the pineapple farm he left the dog to take care of me. I was grateful for him. Our house sits well back from the road, hidden by big trees; an uncomfortable place at night on one's own. But with the dog there

I wasn't troubled by feeling lonely or nervous – he had a ferocious bark. I used to let him stay in the house with me. Going to bed I'd put some music on the record player, and he'd come quietly into the room and curl up on the old armchair. I felt I had good company.

There came a Sunday afternoon in early Spring. I had walked up the two blocks to where our friend Tom (the Head) and his wife Zaida lived, for a yarn and a drink before dinner. I left there in the dusk of a soft, misty evening, lights coming on in the town lying below us in the valley, the fragrance of wattle in the air. It was the time when people were going home to tea, and I was aware of cars on the road.

'Come behind!' I commanded Pablo. He never needed a leash, and he came nicely at my heels. As we walked down the grassy nature strip I kept repeating 'Behind. Stay behind,' and he did.

But a dog is a dog, no matter how well-trained. Close to home we drew level with Freddie Brown's place, and Freddie Brown's dog set up an excited barking. Pablo wheeled on the instant and dashed across the road before I could think – straight under the back wheels of an on-coming car. In terror I saw him give one jerk, and lie still.

Was he dead? Was he dead? Frantic in the middle of the road in the misty dusk I couldn't make myself go close for fear he was broken and bleeding.

The car stopped and an elderly man and woman came up to me, in great distress, saying 'we're so sorry! We just didn't see him.'

'Is he dead? Is he dead? Will you look at him for me?'

The man, much shaken himself, went to him, moved him to the gutter, and came back to me.

'He's breathing his last. Didn't know what hit him. His neck must be broken. He's not knocked about. I think I know him – it's Mr. Whitley's dog, isn't it? I've often seen them together. I wouldn't have hurt him for the world.'

'What'll I do with him? What'll I do?' was all I could think or say.

The unhappy man came with me, stumbling up our long drive in the dark, and I found a couple of sacks. Then back to the road, and he wrapped up our beloved Pablo and brought him to me waiting at the gate. Just a bundle.

'Leave him there under the little pine tree,' I said, 'he'll be all right. I'll ring the Council in the morning and get them to take him away.'

Through the tears that were starting to pour I thanked them, and still telling me they didn't see him and how sorry they were, they went sadly away.

I went inside and called Tom and Zaida. They came rushing down to hold my hand, mop up my tears, and pour me a drink or two. Tom asked me if I would like him to take the body back to their place and keep it there till the morning? I thanked him and said No, he'd be all right where he was under the pine tree. It took a while and a couple of whiskies before I stopped my crazy crying and got myself together, and they felt they could leave me.

I was desolate. Lonely and grieving, and fretting too, about having to tell Whit his dearly loved little mate was dead. I poured some more whisky and cried miserably into my grog. And then – it began to rain. Only a nothing of a dead body, I told myself, but I couldn't bear the thought of it lying out there getting sodden. I rang Tom to take him up on his offer, and he came and took it away.

'I'll get a couple of kids on the job in the morning, and we'll bury him up in the bush – that's what Whit would like don't you think? In the bush where they went for so many walks together.'

Next morning I faced up to school, a sad creature suffering from grief and a hangover. Third period, Remedial English. And there were my six girls, faces full of lively interest, no trace of tension, just a flowing of warmth and sympathy. Words tumbled out of them.

'Oh Mrs. Whitley, we're so sorry your dog's been killed …'

'How did you know about it?'

'The Head came and got Eddie and Wayne out of our class – and they went up in the bush at the back of the school and helped him dig a hole and bury him, at recess. They've just got back …'

'He told us it was a car. Oh poor you!'

'And Mr. Whitley away too!'

'I know what it's like – it's awful. We had a lovely dog, Buster, a big brown dog he was, when he was killed I cried for a week. So did Mum.'

'What you need Mrs. Whitley, is get another dog straight away, that's the best thing.'

'Oh no, I don't think you ought, not for a while, not till you get over it.'

'I think you ought to have a dog there when Mr. Whitley comes home, he'll be too sad if there isn't.'

'I do too.' Was this my surly Leanne? 'I tell you what Mrs. Whitley. I live at Mayfield and there's a lady lives near us, she's got a pup she wants to give away. Look, I'll draw you a map of how to get to our place, and if you come out to Mayfield I'll take you to see her, and I know she'll give him to you. He's a lovely little pup, black and brown.'

'Eddie and Wayne said that they've marked the place where your dog's buried, so you and Mr. Whitley can go and see his grave.'

Tears for another reason came welling into my eyes, but they, bless them, thought it was for the dog.

LETTER TO JO

You were away in England when all this was happening. I suppose my letters reflected my miseries, and you must have grieved for me. I'm sure you'll be interested to know how I got through, and it might come in handy in case the same thing strikes you, or friends of your generation, in say another ten/twenty years.

After Whit came home it was worse than ever. Same old fights, always and ever the same – going back to 'the men being superior to the women', and 'men's work and women's work.' Oh dear, what nonsense it seems now, but Oh dear how it hurt at the time! It was the smart of feeling disregarded, put down, that put the sting in my innards so that I couldn't be sensible. He couldn't stand my unsmiling face, and that there was no laughter, no gaiety any more, let alone any warmth and a bit of a hug and a kiss.

We used to talk about 'selling the house and splitting the proceeds, and each going his own way' – for goodness sake, I was sixty-two and he was sixty-seven – where would we go, how would we live? We never did any more than talk about it, but just lived along a day at a time, each hoping I suppose that 'the wind would change' and the next day wouldn't be so bad.

I think Whit won through by just sticking at it, hanging on tight, doing his own things, playing bowls and watching TV when he wasn't working around house and garden. It was a desolation that our dear old Pablo had been killed and he hadn't had him for company. He used to take great walks on his own, mostly all over the mountain. He was terribly unhappy, and just didn't know where 'I' had gone, what happened to the 'girl' he used to have – the person he loved still. He never glanced at another one. If he ever speaks of that time now he says, 'It's all just a bad dream. I wouldn't know when it was or how long it lasted – it's hard to believe it really happened.'

I think I won through by hunting everywhere, reading every book I could get hold of that might help me, going to Marriage Guidance sessions, talking to women, knowing there must be an answer somewhere, somehow. (I never glanced at another man either – what use would that have been? All to do again.) The biggest helps were Laura Huxley's *You Are Not the Target* and Thomas Harris' *I'm O.K. You O.K.*, which made workable sense to me. They showed how I, Barbara myself, could do something, could go behind what appeared on the surface and look for real values; when words were spoken could work out why, and what they really meant.

There is a Thank-you to go in here, to Margot and Geoff (niece and her husband). They were my sanctuary. I could get on the train and go to them in Melbourne for a few days when a breathing space became absolutely necessary to me. They were unfailingly good and kind to me. Made no questions or comments.

Just accepted me. Their big lounge room had walls lined with books and gramophone records, and I can hear yet the Schubert B Flat piano sonata, which I played over and over and over – it specially solaced my pain at that time.

Help came from outside when you and Garry came home from England, and with you two daughters aged five and three, and a son (as it turned out) on the way. You took up your lives in Melbourne, close enough for frequent visitings, for birthdays and Christmases, and that warmed us up.

Then my beloved eldest brother died. The poor man had been so sick for so long that I couldn't grieve for him; but one does grieve for the finality of it I suppose – that was his life and now it's over, and we who loved him must live on without him. I've felt this since, when dear friends have died after long torment. About then, too, came the first heart attack of my dearly loved friend, Grace. She almost died, and took a long time recovering. This, with Pev's death, gave me to think about my own mortality, and the futility of wasting my one and only good life.

Things began to move a little. My job was exhausting me, after three and a half years, so I retired again. I'd saved like mad, and had enough invested for an income, small – but mine to use as I wanted. I went to Sydney for a holiday, went to the Mitchell Library and looked up the swag of family papers kept there, and got the idea of editing my mum's old diaries into book form. I even got a Special Purposes Grant of $1000 from the Literature Board. I had the diaries photocopied and spent the best part of a year working furiously on them at home. It was great fun. I expected them to be interesting, but I didn't know what a graphic way of writing she had, so rich and yet economical. I have a lovely photograph of her in my study, and often I'd look up at her and say, laughing, 'Good on you, mum!' (These diaries became *The Chronicles of Suzy Em*). I tried various publishers over a period of about two years, and after the sixth rejection I gave up. Then Nan and I decided to have it all photocopied and bound. We had forty copies done, and these have all now been given away to members of the family, to cousins, nephews and nieces, and friends who are interested. I've always been glad I was able to do it, so there it remains, a family treasure).

It was in this year (when I was working on the diaries) that my brother Sep died, and for him I did grieve. He was only sixty-nine and had a lot more life to live; the best part had only started. My brother Septimus. He and Bob were the closest to me in the family, one on either side of me, and always my mates. With them I was safe, secure – no criticism, just love and support no matter what crazy thing I might do (a bit of teasing now and then, sure – plenty). Sep was my special person, always a jump ahead, always teaching me how to do something – climb trees, swim and dive and surf, row a boat, dance, even how to 'roll my own' fags. And always with wise advice at the ready. When we were growing up how we used to talk and talk and talk. Then later on it was my turn to 'pass it on', in my fashion, to Bob.

So I come to one afternoon in early spring of that year. Our friends Mary and John had just bought a house at Anglesea, and told us we'd be happily welcome to borrow it when we fancied. I was thinking about the joy of being by the sea, and about my brother Sep and the sad, sad waste of such a big slab of his life, and his wife's too, that their bitter unhappy marriage was; and the little three years of blissful happiness that came to him towards the end, with his second wife. I was thinking too about the sadness of my two sisters, Lesley and Winsome. Both of them were like princesses to me when I was a schoolgirl, way above me trailing clouds of beauty, brains and boyfriends as they went through university. And now Lesley, imprisoned in her body with crippling arthritis, Winsome imprisoned in her mind after having a brain tumour cut away. And here was I, with no such bad luck, having – and for so long! – this miserable sort of battle with my husband. He happened to come into my room, and before I knew I was going to say it I suggested we take up the kind offer of our friends and go off to the seaside for a week or so. This was proposing the sort of mutuality we hadn't had for years, and he warmed to the idea, but said he couldn't see it working 'without the sex thing'. At which we looked at one another, really looked, and nowadays he says he said it, and I said I did – 'Let's go to bed'. Anyway it was mutual, and so we did, in the middle of a Sunday afternoon. And a jolly good thing too.

We went to Anglesea and had another honeymoon – this time at the ripe ages of seventy-one and sixty-six! I'm not saying it worked like the waving of a magic wand, and all discords disappeared on the instant. But it was a break-through.

And just for fun, on the subject of sex in the over-sixties – your time will come for this, likely, and so you won't be able to say I didn't warn you, here is a piece written some time ago, but still appropriate enough; though the hazards increase with the years.

SEX IN THE OVER-SIXTIES

I found in my book of quotations the other day a charming little verse by Ralph Hodgson called 'Silver Wedding', which is very much to the point of passion after twenty-thirty years have passed and taken with them into limbo most of a person's natural-born exuberance:

> *'Want me and take me for the woman that I am*
> *And not for her that died,*
> *The lovely chit Nineteen I one time was*
> *And am no more,' she cried.*

Back in my jolly old hey-day – my 'lovely chit Nineteen' day – I used to find that the surest way to protect a virtue under siege was to say something funny and make the fellow laugh. Nowadays it is a bird of a different feather. One isn't repelling amorous advances, Oh dear no, *au contraire*. What was once a robust and very hale young amazon who needed skillful curbing is now a sensitive nymph who takes cosseting and cajoling. Laughter is still effective in putting the creature to flight, but mostly these days it is pretty well seasoned with rue and comes just when it isn't wanted. And there are other disaphrodisiacs besides laughter.

Problem One is going-to-bed time. As life rolls along couples commonly find that He and She like to go to bed at different times. She likes to go about ten o'clock and rest her aching back, or feet, or whatever, and have a good read or do the crossword puzzle; and He, after having his doze in front of the TV after dinner, likes to stay up and watch until it closes down. Just when

She's happily half-asleep and reaching to switch the light off, Himself comes in, wakes her well and truly as he thumps about getting his clothes off and his pyjamas on and lands heavily in the bed with newspaper in hand, saying he'll only be ten minutes. Herself can't go to sleep when the light's on, and so she suffers for the ensuing half hour and is a lump of cranky temper when he puts the light out at last and stretches his connubial arm over. The nymph has no show at all. But when Herself is asleep and the light out when he comes in, he tiptoes about and gentles his shoes onto the floor and his body onto the bed. And this time when he stretches his arm over she turns to him all sleepy and reciprocal; but she has to scrabble under the pillow for her hanky, sit up and have a good blow of the nose, and then find her nasal drops. De-reciprocation all round.

Problem Two is the wretched way the body won't behave itself, and stabs its owner with aches and pains at unexpected and critical moments. Perhaps the nymph has been solicited and comes doucely to heel; she doesn't like it when someone says 'Look out for my sore shoulder,' 'you're hurting my neck,' 'I forgot to take my pill,' or, worst of all being seized with violent cramp, yells 'Ow!, my leg!' By the time the afflicted party gets out of bed, stamps on the floor and massages the offender for ten minutes, and gets back, He-or-She can find the nymph elsewhere and the spouse fast asleep. (But leaving this fugitive wench out of the discussion for the moment, there are comforts to be had for uncomfortable bodies, the warming up of cold feet for instance, and I know more than one woman who speaks very highly of the solace of a good, solid, warm masculine rump placed strategically against the aching hollow of a feminine back.)

Problem Three is to do with food, and what there was for dinner, like curry maybe. The greatest dis-aphrodisiac of them all is the mighty attack of wind. Not quite so disastrous when it gives due warning, and time to leap out of bed with a 'Sorry Love', and out into the passage (or breezeway as one couple I know have named it). But when it breaks forth with no notice of intent, and there is wincing and holding of the nose, the nymph is off and away like magic.

Problem Four is about drink, and the quantity and quality of liquid intake during the evening. This same couple I know haven't had 'relations' of a Friday night for many, many years, Friday (as all good Aussie-aussie wives know) being sacred to the Boys in the Pub, and Himself tied to the ritual of coming home slightly sloshed. The nymph knows her place of a Friday, and that she is safely tucked away there for the night. No need to quote the famous words of the Porter in *Macbeth* about alcohol provoking the desire and taking away the performance — this is something we all know very well, and Herself isn't averse to a noggin or two on occasion either. But what about next morning? As if for revenge the nymph is capable of getting a bit on the bold side, and taking a nasty joy in making her presence felt when there's no hope of appeasing her until there have been trips to the bathroom for the cleaning of teeth and the sweetening of breath — meanwhile the fickle wench nicks off again.

Problem Five is the domestic discussion. Though the children have long since flown the nest, He and She stick to the habit made when they were still within it, and wait till bed-time to talk over things that need to be talked over. And such is life in the Over-Sixties the silly couple talk it over first instead of after, and — not always, but Oh how often — end up lying back to back each on the limit of accommodation on opposite edges of the bed, and cringing from contact as from the fires of hell and Satan's very pitchfork itself.

Not that this phenomenon is peculiar to life in the sixties; it is a corollary of married life from the start, and you might think that couples grow out of it in time, but they don't; and the only real solution to this and other discordances is the drastic one of twin beds, or one party taking to the bed in the spare room. And as for that, when Ogden Nash was discussing the relative merits of bath or shower he said he wouldn't enter any argument about it, only say that there are three things you can't do in a shower, and one is read and one is smoke and the other is get wet all over. So I say nothing about the merits of sleeping in separate beds except that there are three things you can't do in peace in a double one, and one is snore and one is scratch and the other is enjoy a nice bag of toffees.

But single beds or a double one, times do turn up when all the dis-aphrodisiacs are absent; all the pills have been taken, the anti-cramp exercises done, a simple grilled chop has been eaten for dinner and a modicum of liquor partaken; perfect amity prevails about having parlour painted, and the nymph is graciously benign; and as our Over-Sixty couple are lying cosily in what Dr. Marie Stopes so sweetly called 'the afterglow', Himself says, 'You know, this is very pleasant — why don't we do it more often?'

9. Moving Out of the Doldrums

Our lives jogged along, and slowly, slowly, we came together. We still had a spat now and then, but I'd learned my lessons and could lean on my sure knowledge, for one – 'kindness is all'.

In all our miserable time of conflict Whit was unfailing in his kindness and generosity to members of my family when any of them came our way, or needed our care. And so was I to his (I mind me of my mum, long ago, and the unspoken pact that no matter what was awry I'd always be around to do her hair). When Jo and the family came back from England this gave Whit more open doors for his kindness to flow through. He never can resist little kids anyway, and he let it flow over and around them well and truly. Whenever they came to stay, which at first was at Easter and Christmas with their dad and mum, and later on their own in school holidays, always they had 'an adventure with Whit'. Just the three with him – no other adults allowed – and away they'd go, out in the bush, climbing up the mountain, scrambling round the old volcano to see an eagle's nest – some surprise. And back they'd come with shining eyes still knowing wide spaces. Lucy said to me once, when she was eleven or so, 'I don't know anybody, not *anybody* who has a Grandpa anything *like* as good as Whit.'

I love to remember one Easter morning seven years ago, when just for once I was included. The children were eleven, nine and nearly six, and Whit gathered them to him saying he'd been worrying about the adventure this time, because he was to play bowls over the weekend. The only time he could think of was Sunday morning when he wasn't due at the green until 10 o'clock, so what if we got up very early and he'd drive us out to see the sunrise from the top of the mountain? Eyes sparkled. The sun was to rise at six-thirty, so we'd have to get up about five-thirty – they could take their Easter eggs along and have them up on the mountain top. Eyes, faces, and even bodies sparkled at this bit of a plan.

Easter was early in April. Out of bed in the dark, throw clothes on, grab coats, find some apples, collect dog, and we're off.

It was lovely just driving through the quiet town and out along the road, the lights of the car picking out trees and farm houses. As we went up the mountain-side the dawn was lightening and we could see the shapes of the great rocks and the old, old gum trees. But when we arrived at the flat rocky space at the top, Oh what a blow! There was another car there! And a group of young people just in the exact sheltered spot Whit had in mind. So we had to find ourselves another, with a fine big boulder at our backs because of the chilly little wind that was blowing up from the gently-folding pasture land to the east. So we got cosy, Lucy (the cold one) snugged up in front of me, and looked away over the flats to where the light was growing brighter and brighter on the horizon, waiting for the very moment when the sun would show itself.

And then. A lovely, wonderful thing – the sound of music – bagpipes playing 'Amazing Grace'. We looked across to the group of young folks, and there was a piper in full Scottish rig, in slow pace piping the sun up on Easter morning. And – 'There it is!

There it is!' The glowing flame-red arc came over the edge of the world, swelled up into its orb and went slowly behind a belt of blue-grey cloud and out again. I can hear Lucy's voice yet, soft, hushed by the magic. 'Isn't it beautiful – isn't it ... beautiful!'

The piper kept playing hymn music and the sunlight changed the look of our landscape, twinkling the leaves of the great gum trees, glinting their trunks, bringing us back to everyday. And the children – 'Can we have our Easter eggs now?' So we made back to the car. We were met there by one of the young group, very charming, asking would we care to join them in their fellowship? 'Thank you lad,' I said, 'we feel we have.'

Another door opening for Whit's affection and fun was when we got a new dog. We hadn't had one for four years since our dear old fellow was killed, and it was a sure sign that our 'mutuality' was growing again that we decided to get one. This chap came from the Animal Aid people, about a year old, and a frightened little soul he was. Terrified of a rake, fork, tea-towel – anything in one's hand; we felt sure he'd been belted. It took a long time to reassure him. Whit's procedure with a dog is to be merciless in his training until the poor animal is completely obedient; and then the fun starts. It was a door for me too. It was good to have the little creature around and about, and good for my vigour and figure as well, because my self-appointed job was his morning walk, round the block.

Our lives altered too in that there were many calls on our compassion. Lonely people for a start. George was left alone, and then Tom, and when we met Alan his wife had recently died. Whit's sisters were growing old, and so was my Nan. Some of our younger friends had massive troubles. I used to think there was one thing about retirement that no-one seems to mention – a person is available, no longer going to work. Time and time again there was a need for our ears, hands, feet and fingers, and in our response we were sure of each other. A sudden call on the phone, say from Tom who'd had a black-out and crashed onto the kitchen floor, and I could say, 'Whit will be up in a few minutes,' and no need to ask him.

Another lesson I'd learned, and properly, was – I'll quote Donne again:

> *To our bodies turn we then, that so*
> *Weak man on love revealed may look,*
> *Love's mysteries in souls do grow;*
> *But yet the body is his book.*

Sure, sex in the sixties hasn't the urgency it used to have, or the frequency either, but it's still 'sugar and spice and everything nice,' and it's a marvellous dissolver of tensions. I don't know which is the chicken and which is the egg, as far concerns both of us being remarkably fit and well for the ages we are, and still being 'sexually active' (to use a clinical phrase).

One thing perhaps above all. It was the next year after our reconciliation. We had a calendar in the kitchen, with a lovely photograph of sand, waves and sea, and one day I was looking at it with such longing – I, the poor expatriate Sydney-sider and surf-lover – that Whit joined me and we decided to pack up the car and go northwards in the winter, to look for our beloved spot on the NSW coast that we'd found in our after-retirement holiday, and see if by any unlikely chance it was still unspoilt. And when we did, it was hardly changed since seven years! Almost too good to be true. We took a little flat and refreshed our hearts and bodies with a month of wonderful holiday. We mucked about on all-to-ourselves beaches and rockhoppy headlands, watched waves rolling and crashing and tossing, lay on hot sand in the sun, surfed; had our evening beer sitting in the car outside the pub, watching the sunset reflected in the peaceful river; had paw-paw for breakfast and fish for dinner. All of these things both of us love so much, it was a true bringing together of separated spirits.

LETTER TO MYSELF

It's interesting to see how the whole pattern of my life changed after the 'breakthrough'. The next year my two closest friends died, within six months. My two dear friends. How lucky I was to have them. Grace, the gently loving darling, compound of care and tenderness (stitched up with guts); and Joan, with her passion for truth, honesty and justice, her brain like a keen-edged rapier, and many's the cut she dealt with it, to friends and all, me included. I'd thought I'd be in a desolation of loneliness without them, but strangely life compensated me by producing new friends and activities.

I had more time to look out for them, perhaps, now I wasn't wasting so much of it in the despondency of marriage discord. I went along to the local Education Centre and offered myself for any voluntary work they might have. 'Time on your hands?' the Director asked me. 'Not exactly,' I said, 'it's that I'm not involved in anything outside the four walls of home.' He asked me to do some 'oral history' interviews for their monthly publication. The first was with a fine old man, come from England when he was eighteen and an expert worker in mines all his life, and I enjoyed it immensely. Then I did a series of such interviews with another wonderful person, a dear little lady over ninety, who had lived in Castlemaine since she was born and was chock-a-block with history. I enjoyed this immensely too.

Then I saw an advertisement in the local paper, almost too good to be true. A young couple, fond of opera, willing to share their collection of records and their fine quality instrument with anyone interested. 'Opera,' say I to myself, 'that's one branch of music I don't know anything about – except for *La Boheme* and *Carmen*. Here's my chance!' And away I went. Oh it was lovely! In winter time we started, eight or so people sitting round a blazing log fire with librettos in our hands, concentrating while the gorgeous music filled the room – *Fidelio, Falstaff, Rigoletto* – Oh! There was a table before us with sherry and tasty goodies on it to refresh us between acts, and much talk afterwards, our hostess perhaps playing some of the arias sung by various artists for our comparison. I certainly found there was more in opera than I'd dreamed of. We met once a month. I went by myself, and made new friends. The group ran on for two years or so before kids and responsibilities got too much for our host and hostess. Thanks to them for ever for so much pleasure.

Came along another good thing. Friend George, after his beloved Grace died, was a lonely lonely man. He used to come to us once a week for dinner and three-handed Solo, and went to other friends as well. In the return he felt he must make, he offered to share an expertise he had, and teach us to play Bridge. I resisted for a while, not enticed by what I knew of Bridge players, with all their protocol and dire seriousness, but one night, somewhat in my cups if I remember, I said I was about ready to learn to play; so I was added to a group of four and made one over, and George was free to instruct. This arrangement didn't last long. George went back to England after some weeks, and never came back to Australia. He died during that year, dear George. But we've kept up the Bridge nights, with more laughter than protocol, more fun than seriousness. Thank you, George, thank you!

Then another fine thing. The Melbourne Theatre Company (MTC) started a scheme of special concessions for country people, with a free bus. We had to book for a certain number of plays each season. Whit wasn't interested in going but I jumped at it. Get the bus at six p.m., take some nourishment or maybe a bottle of wine or a thermos, and after the show the bus would be waiting at the door. We'd get home about one in the morning. Saw some good shows and some so-sos, but it was a good night anyway with the talking on the bus, especially going over the show on the way back. I really made friends with Alan on these trips. With Lorna too, which led me on to one of the best things happening in my life right now.

I'd been asked by the Education Centre people if I'd take a course for them in Creative Writing. 'No way in the world am I competent to do any such thing,' said I, 'But I'd undertake a workshop, perhaps, folk bringing their work along for criticism and discussion.' Then I was smitten by diffidence, and doubt that I could handle it. So I asked Lorna (a writer of poetry) what she thought of the notion, and said she 'I'd be in that! I'd help you.' So we started it off. We gave over the Workshop after one term, and have carried it on as a writer's group between ourselves, with comers and goers, up to now.

I kept with the MTC trips for a couple of years, and then we had the chance to join the Bendigo Film Society, to which Alan belonged, and in this Whit was interested, so it was a thing we could share. Alan comes to dinner and off we go, Whit driving, when there's a film that interests us, and provided we aren't committed to something else. We see some superb films, and I think we've had five really worthwhile weekend festivals.

All in all, lucky lucky me. My regrets are all for my own shortcomings, except the old one that I couldn't help – the more-than-one-children that I wished for. I could be rueful about the times when I wasted patches of my one and only good life, the year I spent crying over Clarrie for instance (aged twenty-two), but the years of 'sorry time' especially, though I suppose it helps me to be understanding and non-critical nowadays when I'm coping with the burden of someone else's troubles. And all that nonsense of the blokes-and-bosses time when I could/should have been getting stuck into some worthwhile job in life, or at least learning to play the piano – or a squeezebox now, wouldn't that have been fun all along! Wouldn't the mentally retarded kids have loved that! I've had music, had to have it, but only to listen to; I didn't study it, don't know enough about it. Which is true of other things I love. I can read – the knowledge is there waiting for me, and I haven't grabbed it. Trees for instance, birds, gardens, creatures. All I can do now is be grateful for TV and record my thanks to all the splendid nature programs, to David Attenborough in particular and his wonderful *Living Planet*.

What of the physical woman during all this time? My hair went grey, my few remaining teeth were yanked out, my body changed in shape and so did my face. I was constrained to do something about my hair (my last remaining vanity) by a sister-in-law's remark one time when I was visiting Sydney. 'Why don't you put a rinse through it?' she said, 'You used to have such pretty hair.' Oh dear Oh dear. So experiment with bottles of stuff from the chemist's shop, and find a damned nuisance of a 'rinse' that is discreet and (I hope) looks natural. What a pest it is! Takes me an hour-and-a-half to wash and fix my hair. Won't I rejoice when it goes beautifully silver like my mum's, or sister Nan's.

As for the teeth! Ach … ugh! I happened to read an article in the paper not long after this catastrophe, which said a thing I entirely agree with: 'Life's three fates are birth, death and total dentures.' The for-years-continuing visits to the dentist, the relinings, the relievings of pressure on the wretched ulcers! The forgoing of favourite foods, like celery and blackberry jam on toast. And apples! Oh, Oh, Oh! Never again the delight of chomping the teeth into a rich red apple just off the tree, and the juice running down the chin. Have to cut it into little bits and pop them in. Or grate it – what a sin! And I live in apple country!

The shape of my face I could do nothing about – it's a thin face, and that's all about it. As for the ageing body – I used to think that a woman can turn into a fat old lady or a thin old lady, but I was likely to be a skinny old lady with a fat tummy. And this I am. The poor arms and legs get skinnier and skinnier, and the tummy more and more of a podge. I have the devil of a hunt for loose dresses with no waistline. I suppose it started in the Mildura days, when the only assuaging drink in a raging heatwave was an ice-cold beer. And then another. My appetite for beer settled in.

But for all this, twenty-seven years in Castlemaine and heaven knows how many visits to friends in hospital; even Whit was there for ten days years ago when he had sciatica, with his legs in traction after a 'violent adjustment', but me – not one day or night have I had to spend there. I'm not complaining, no indeed.

Going to Writer's Group I felt constrained to take material of my own, so I opened up my typewriter again. It was a lovely feeling of familiarity, like meeting an old friend, but I didn't know where to start, after ten years. When I was in Senior years in High School we had a splendid teacher for English, and I thank her for ever for introducing me to the enjoyment of our literature. Her lessons were a delight – 'magic moment' stuff – but I also owe her a negative. When it came to our own writing she impressed on us, vehemently, that we could only write well about what we knew. If only, once a month say, she'd set us to a sheer flight of imagination! I was just beginning to learn the art of beginning with the base of a real happening and concocting it into a story when I closed down the typewriter in the 'sorry years'. So, starting off again I went back to scratch and wrote about something I know very well, and love very much.

ESSAY FOR MISS M

Morning Walk

Off I go, every day that I'm home and hale, with my little dog. From the front gate we look down over the town with its greenery, always beautiful to see, but I love it especially when there's a mist and the houses lie under the greyness and poke up a chimney here and there, with a drift of smoke, and the gum trees and elms in the hollow, feet hidden, hold up their heads breathing a delicate quiet dignity.

Dog and I always walk to the corner of one crossroad, and then to the next where we leave the going-to-work traffic to its busy and smelly devices, and turn into a secluded almost secret piece of dirt road, broad with a lovely lofty gum tree fair in the middle and private deep-gardened houses either side. One of my favourite kinds of morning is when the shapes are softened by the mist and there's no sound but a faint drip from green-growing things. There are other magic mornings, frosty, clear and crisp, with not a cloud in all the wide sky, just a soft haze of grey-blueness over the mountain top across the valley. Often I stop and stand under the lofty gum-tree and look up at the blue sky, so profoundly blue seen through the bunchy leafiness. It's a very old tree with a rough knobbly trunk and two great wide-spreading arms. The leaves slight and silvery stir gently in the morning air, and sometimes hosts of tiny green finches go singing and flying everywhere among the branches, so that the whole tree-top seems to be alive with dancing movement.

Next we turn right again and up the hill, round the corner and so by another dirt road home. Always the same way. It's important that I see the gardens and trees in exactly the same perspective and pattern every time, I'm not quite sure why. I'm like a kid being read a familiar fairy story and not one word or sequence must be altered.

There are folk in cars going downwards to the town or upwards to the Primary School, maybe I know them and maybe I don't, but they wave to me and I wave back. Even the folk in the houses must notice me going by. A woman in a garden, whom I'd never seen before, said her very first words to me: 'You're later than usual this morning.'

There are kids riding their bikes to school and kids walking, ambling, mooching, meandering, stone-kicking and chatter-yabbering along towards me on the top dirt road – peripatetic flowers with their pretty faces and bright clothes. They smile and say 'Hullo' or 'G'day', sometimes very shy because they know they don't really know me. But the dog they know because I've told them his name, and he gets joyful greetings of 'Hullo Rowley!' and nice soft pats. They say 'See ya' and on they go.

Rain, hail, shine, furious frost or hectic heat, I can't miss my walk, and why is because of the mighty emotional blackmail put on by the scrap of pooch. When he gives me the full works with the melting brown eyes and the beseeching little yelpy sounds, I tell you, there's no way in the world I could knock him back.

I'm part of the morning scenery to all who live or go that way. In winter when I needs must put on woolly socks, fleecy-lined boots, heavy slacks, three jumpers, a coat and a cover-the-ears scarf and I can't even see because the gale from the Antarctic is making my eyes stream, I wonder if my public is thinking, 'There goes the mad old woman of Farley Street.' But when I come home, no matter what outrageous tantrum the weather might have been putting on, I'm grateful to that small hound. I feel I've made friends with the day.

Sometimes Maisie would come with us, when she was well enough. I'm sure we used to get at least as much pleasure out of people's gardens as they did themselves. We knew every tree on our way and loved to look for the change and turn of limbs and leaves in the slow pace of seasons. They were all our friends. The great scarlet oak at the first corner, round to the right and right again, the huge spreading golden elm and the dark red crab apple in the garden opposite. Up the hill a row of liquidambers in the nature strip on one side and gum trees on the other, a silver birch and a fine copper beech behind a low fence, and facing us on the hill-top two autumn-gorgeous claret ashes. Turning the last corner we went past back fences, and there branches lean over. A red bottle-brush is one. When it's in full flurry and the morning sun is shining through you can see me standing underneath, adoring. There's a Hardenbergia, right along a fence. Maisie and I would watch the buds come, long before spring got going, and rejoice in the very first flower that opened, and soon after, the rollicking purple abundance.

One back yard has four fine wattle trees, all different, and they flower separately between August and December. One of them has slim, delicate leaves and a pale golden flower that comes out about Christmas time. I snitched some of its seeds one autumn, just for fun. I'm no expert at growing natives, but I planted them as advised by one who is, and – such pride! – I accomplished three strong little plants. One I gave to our daughter, one I planted in our poor old stony garden, and one I gave to friend Alan. He lives in a house I pass by every morning, and he planted his in the nature strip in front. The little tree said gaily, 'This'll do me,' and has been growing very cheerfully there ever since. Alan confesses that he leaves it alone to make its own arrangements, and doesn't bother it with watering or any fuss. I tell it Hullo, of course, as I go by.

But four years ago a dreadful sadness came over my green-growing friends, many of them. When we came home in August from a six-week holiday they'd been stricken by drought and dire frosts, and were standing there lifeless, with crackly brown leaves.

Sue's beautiful glowing lemon tree and her enormous white daisy bush, the Brown's tall Virgilia, the old peppercorn down by the creek, Edna's passionfruit vine all over her chookhouse, the Hardenbergia on the fence – all, all stark dead.

Morning walk had lost its magic for me, even in the sweet spring weather, even with the pink and white blossom trees miraculously abloom, even with the clear blue sky – blue sky! Never would I have dreamt that I'd hate the sight of it. Barefaced, blatant, day after day, cruel blue sky. Weeks and weeks went by; long since the grass had died and dried away to nothing; fruit from the blossom trees had shrivelled and dropped; the gum trees were lank and listless and their pale dead leaves lay all about on the sad earth; here and there were fallen branches. On some few days – and Oh for the heart lifting! – grey clouds, clearly chock-a-block with rain, would come looming over us. They'd drop three spits and a dribble and roll away behind the mountain. We still went on our walk, Rowley and I and sometimes Maisie. But where had the magic gone? The spirit of the place that used to speak to me and make me friends with the day, when would it ever come back?

By December, when Maisie came, we were only doing half the walk, keeping on the flat. On Christmas eve she didn't come, so Rowley and I did the full walk up the hill and round the corner, which we hadn't done for a while. And what do you think! Would you believe it! Alan's little wattle tree, that I grew from a seed, now taller than I was – it was all a-blossom with soft pale flowers, tossing its fine leaves and wafting its fresh perfume blithely in the breeze!

Maybe we will have rain again some day, even soon, I thought.

MAISIE

What can I say of my little friend Maisie? Who lived not far away at the bottom of the hill where we lived at the top, and who used to teach at the same school where Whit and I did? It is four years ago this week since she died, and perhaps I can now put into shape the memories that come pelting at me when I think of her, which is very often.

I could start with one evening, years back in the 'sorry time' when Whit was away in Queensland and I had been living with only our dog for company and protection. It was just a few days after he'd been killed on the road, and in my grief for him I'd been smitten with a knock-out dose of the 'flu. I was sitting by the fire with a beer and some egg on toast, feeling utterly, utterly lonely, sick and unhappy. And to the back door came Maisie, 'to see how you are'. Her kindness undid me and let loose the tears in a torrent. She gathered me up, with my nightie and toothbrush, took me home with her and put me to bed. Somehow she managed to nurse me through weeks of wretched sickness, buying and lumping home the oranges, brandy and Disprin I was living on, but trying to find food that would tempt me to eat, putting Beethoven on the radiogram to soothe me, and of course going to work every day. It was one time, I think looking back, when I should have spent a few days in the hospital, but I simply didn't think of getting a doctor to put me there. And neither did she.

So many memories of her! All of us who knew her would say, 'What about her and all that jam!' Growing up in the Depression time she'd been very poor as a child and in her young married life, very very poor, and was still incapable of wasting food, any foodstuff at all. From January to March, abundance time, the stockpot was always bubbling on her stove – plums, apricots, peaches, apples, tomatoes, quinces, crab apples, blackberries – into jams, sauces, jellies. She never threw out the rinds of grapefruit and oranges – too good a base for a little pot or two of marmalade. So well known was she for this activity that just as she thought say quinces were all over she'd come home some evening and find a beer carton full of them sitting on her doorstep. 'More quinces!' she'd exclaim, just about ready to weep, but such a pained, incredulous look she'd give me if I said, 'Haven't you heard of throwing stuff onto a compost heap?'

Some of this bottled bounty she'd give away to friends, family, to the Home for the Aged; some of it she sold to teachers at the school in aid of the Red Cross; and some she stored on her pantry shelves, which had been built to size especially to hold these bottles, and looked, when full, like a neat and variegated little library. And by the next January it would all be gone. She never went to anyone's house for a visit without her basket on her arm and some of her 'apricot and pineapple, and apple marmalade, for you to try.' Children visiting her (many and often) were invited into the pantry to have a pick.

She lived on her own, mostly, when I knew her, except when her children, grandchildren or friends came to stay. She didn't drive a car, and many's the time when I, or someone, would stop and pick her up laden with bulging shopping baskets and drive her home. After she retired, which was three years after I did, she said that one nice thing she could do is come on the morning walk with me and the dog (we had a new one by then). So I'd call for her on my way, and off we'd go and then we'd make arrangements for shopping if she wanted something 'down the street'. It was a bit of a royal progress, she'd be stopped at least on every corner by a person who wanted to chat. She'd lived most of her life in Castlemaine, gone to Primary and High School here, and always to church, and then she'd taught here too, so she had myriad friends who all loved her dearly, so loving was she herself. I was going to say she was never critical, but in one respect she jolly well was. She'd get very hostile (talking to me, not to them) about young mothers who went back to work when they should have been at home looking after their children. She'd rage. Her values were the simple, honest, old-fashioned ones.

The morning walk became a ritual, and I realise now I'd never had a friend like she was, ever before. We'd share all the little things of everyday – we'd have someone coming in for lunch on Friday, or the family on Sunday, and what we planned to cook for them; the first gladiolus was showing colour; cauliflowers were cheap enough for the making of pickles; the good, bad or funny doings of grandchildren; the need for new shoes and where Oh where to buy them; she was just running up a new dress for the Social tomorrow. The stuff of life.

She was just a wonder about people. On our walk she not only knew who lived in every house we passed, she knew their life stories, the woman's name before she married, the man's job, how many children there were and how they turned out. Of half the population of the town, it seemed to me, she knew the histories, who had been naughty and played up in their young days, who'd had to get married and how long that marriage lasted, when a baby was coming – and up to the hospital with Maisie when he/she arrived, bearing a present and a card. As for Christmas cards, she gave and received dozens and dozens, and loved to decorate her living room with festoons of them. She loved everything to do with Christmas, every bit of the ritual and custom. When my sister Nan was ever staying with us then, Maisie came in very handy as someone she could go to church with.

Meeting a lass going to the Primary School in the mornings, it'd be 'Hullo Leanne,' and then I'd hear 'Her mother was Betty Bilson, she married one of the Turner boys.' Another thing she decided to do after she retired was go once a week to this school and give Religious Education, so she was *au fait* with all the little ones.

She never came home from our walk with empty hands. A couple of pine cones perhaps, a flower or some shivery grass, fallen sticks from the gum trees to kindle her fire. She had an electric stove (where the stock pots bubbled), but she loved her old one-fire stove better. She lit it first thing every morning and I used to wonder at all the things remotely burnable in household rubbish that were poked into that fire, and how in the world it kept burning. Later, when she was sick, I'd look for the smoke from her chimney and know whether she was up and about or still in bed.

The story of her illness was a long and sad one, but I'll be brief about it. It began with pains in the stomach, trips to doctors and hospitals, tests and checkups, and then somehow, without her exactly telling us, we knew she had cancer. She put herself in the medicos hands and did as she was bid; I remember how she scorned and hated the barrage of pill bottles in her kitchen, but she took them. It was all hell. Then poor little soul was going to Melbourne by ambulance every two weeks for chemotherapy; she couldn't say what they did to her or why, but clearly it was unspeakable torment and torture. All her hair came out, and she was marvelous about that and the whole doings. She had a gift for telling us, her friends, what she'd been through without complaining – even with humour. I'd call in every morning to see how she was, and we were both delighted if she felt well enough to join in the walk. She loved to do it if she could, but sometimes she only just made it. We did a short one, round the block on the flat, and I remember still the gardens there in that last summer of Maisie's life. When Number 10 put his pansies in, how quickly they flourished and flowered; the lush roses in Number 12, how tempted we were to snitch a bud or two hanging over the fence; the multitudinous petunias in Number 14, how gaily they grew and blazed with colour; how longingly we looked at the beans, the silver beet and cabbage in Number 16; how the zinnias in Number 18 seemed to leap from sturdy little plants to masses of brilliant colour; how dazzling the green lawn in Number 20 among all the others burnt away during the drought, because this house had a well of its own down the back. All these stay the same, fixed and unchanging in my memory. I don't walk that way anymore.

She had quite a good remission towards the end of the year. She even went on a pleasant bus tour to Eden with a friend, Anne, and in spite of everyone's fears, including her own, was able to manage all the sitting and the eating without too much trouble. And she enjoyed her Christmas. But then she became Oh so sick! With nausea, then diarrhoea and vomiting. She could hardly eat anything, and it was distressing to see her getting thinner and thinner. The vile hot steamy weather was exhausting to us hale and hearty ones, and she found it hard to endure indeed. At least she didn't have to wear her heavy uncomfortable wig – her hair had grown quite a bit when she was taken off the chemotherapy. Her hosts of friends called in constantly, which was her greatest pleasure, as she found it hard to fill up her days. Her doctor had told her that if she couldn't manage on her own he'd put her into hospital 'for a rest', and it was a relief to us all when she decided to go there.

A lovely peace came to her then, when she stopped battling and allowed herself to be looked after. There wasn't a nurse in the town who didn't know and love her, and they cherished her very tenderly and kept her out of pain as best they could. Friends came in thick and fast to see her, family too (though none of her four children lived in Castlemaine), and I think she was happy. It was only on Wednesday, the day before she died, that she went right down and there was no strength left in the little body at all. She didn't know it was a day to become famous, Ash Wednesday itself, and that her son and his family living in Woodend were threatened by the fires.

The next day I went up in the afternoon. Anne was there, and she soon left. I stayed a while. Maisie was finding it hard to talk, so I said 'Don't try. I'll just sit here and you'll know I'm here and I love you.' She kept dozing off, rather it was wafting away, and then she'd open her eyes and say 'I've been in another world.' She knew she was dying, and so did I. You couldn't imagine anything so gentle, so serene and simple. She said 'It's been a good way hasn't it, being here?' Meaning a good way to depart. We talked a little bit. I said 'It comes to us all, darling.' 'Yes,' she said. 'When God is ready for us,' I said. 'Yes,' she said, 'that's it.' I sat a while holding her hand and watching her slipping away. She came back again and said 'I'm pretty low, aren't I?' 'Yes, darling,' I said. 'They won't expect me to get over this, will they, the family, and go back and get on with things?' 'No darling,' I said. I can see her little face so clearly still, can see her going and coming back, and her serene acceptance of the fact of death. She made it a natural, simple thing, for me: I don't think I'll be afraid of it myself anymore. I always have been afraid of becoming nothing. She died about two hours after I left her. Meg had been in to see her after I went, so she had three close friends there that afternoon.

She had none of the family. Life was made very complicated for them by the bush fires. Her son Laurie and his wife Fay had to evacuate their house at Woodend, and had brought their two children up here and into Anne's charge about six that morning and had to dash straight back. Laurie was fire-fighting and Fay had to keep her eye on the house (which escaped being burnt, just) for fear of looters. The hospital had been trying to get in touch with her daughter Alison, but she was driving on her way up here, and was held up by the fires.

The funeral service was sincere and simple; the church was so full there were many standing; the flowers were heaped high. I had tearful kisses and grasps of the hand from people I barely knew, people who'd seen us together so often walking in the mornings. But I'd said my Goodbye, her torment was over, and I couldn't grieve.

Such a strange thing. When Grace died, and six months later Joan, in both cases I had a great sense of loss. They both went away, right away, wherever they went. I didn't feel like that with Maisie. I wasn't conscious of her actual presence, but I felt she was still very much around, in her home, in the streets where we walked, in the town, especially in the Gardens where the lovely rose beds are. People said things to me: 'You'll miss her,' 'It's a great loss,' and such, and I wanted to say 'What are you talking about?'

But I think she's gone now, and now I do miss her.

10. Come Elements of Youth and Age

I first met my granddaughters in Oxford in 1972, after I retired for the first time and took myself to England. It was eight years since Jo and Garry had left Australia, and they'd been through a lot of intense and often difficult living in that time. I was in a rare state of excitement when I landed at Heathrow and saw the four of them waiting behind the barrier. The ache in my arms to be assuaged at last!

I found out very quickly there was more to Anna than a pretty darling little girl. To this day it's hard for me to imagine where they got that one from, such a stormy petrel she was then, is now, and probably always will be. Chock-a-block with energy, abilities, brains, ideas, imagination, stingo; and at that time suffering from the frustrations of being only three and a half and not big enough, not old enough, to read, write, go for walks on her own, do so many things! Lucy was one and a half and still a baby, but even then clearly a much less forceful person.

The family was barely living on a slender grant, in a pokey flat that was part of an old house converted for student living. It had two bedrooms, a bathroom-cum-laundry, and one all-purpose room that had a slice cut out of it for a miniscule kitchen; up two flights of winding stairs, and the door always closed because Lucy could have fallen all the way down. How the children hated that closed door!

LETTER TO ANNA

You were a caged tigress. If we went out in the ramshackle car, when we came home that door would be looming. Problem one was getting you out of the car; two was catching you when you cleared off, and getting you inside the front door; three was getting you up those awful stairs, Jo with Lucy and shopping bags to negotiate, and you hollering blue murder. You hollered a lot of the time the six months I stayed in Oxford (in a little bedsitter I was lucky enough to find). Already I think Lucy must have been refusing to compete, or else she was like her mum, by nature silent. She didn't even utter sweet baby talk. But if I produced the magic word 'walk' she'd into the bedroom as if on wheels and be back pronto with her red cape and hood. She was a tiny thing and looked like a pixie.

 I was often taking you both for walks, to the famous Parks, which were close to where you lived; Lucy in the pusher, you never but never alongside – way ahead, or behind, doing your own investigations, and I'd be hauling you out of people's gardens half the time. Arrived at the Parks you'd take charge and push Lucy off for a make-up game of your own, and Grannie had to sit down somewhere and keep out of the way.

 How you loved to sing! When Jo took us out for drives to show me charming English villages you were always in a fidget, boxed up in the back of the car. So Jo would start you off with 'Old Macdonald Had a Farm', and then you'd be right, you'd sing all the way, sing, sing, sing, one nursery rhyme after another. I could hardly believe such a little thing could know so many, and sing so truly.

Dancing you both loved. I used to find kid-stuff records in a music shop. If you were hollering your head off and saw me lift the lid of the player you'd stop on the instant. I'm sure you hollered rather than be bored.

Getting you to bed! Jo'd do Lucy and I'd do you, when Garry was out, and I always had to have a puppet, finger game, toy, to take your attention while I got your clothes off, and about three nappies onto your solid young bottom; you'd started wetting the bed in jealousy of Lucy, who was still being breast-fed. One night I looked at you, little squirming yelling creature, and said 'Oh Anna! I'm too tired tonight to think of a gimmick for you …', and on inspiration, with my tongue I shoved my bottom denture out between my lips. Fascinated silence! It was the best trick yet – stopped you in mid-holler.

Sometimes, to give Jo a bit of peace, I'd take you for a ride on a bus, upstairs on a double-decker, to a park where there was a playground, and I'd hope to use up some of your overflowing energy on the slippery slide, the climbing frame, and, over and over again, the swing. We'd have the place to ourselves till half-past-three, and then you'd have lots of company. The park was next door to a Primary School, and the kids would tumble out when school was over and rush across for some fun and exercise before they went home. You thought this was great, and you'd be friends with someone in the first five minutes. And then, little wretch, there were only two ways to get you off and over to the bus stop – brute force or bribery, and we both preferred the latter. I'd be forearmed with a treat in my bag, some sweets or a packet of potato chips. They would last you all the way home.

It's funny to think you probably don't remember anything of our Oxford doings, and yet they're etched clear and sharp in my memory.

NEW ELEMENTS ~ GRANDCHILDREN

The time came when I had to leave them to battle it out on their own, and return to Australia. It was two and a half years later when Garry, his degree accomplished, landed a job at Monash and they came back home again.

We were very much involved with the young family then, and they certainly needed some back-stopping. Taking up life again in Melbourne after so long away, almost broke, finding a house to live in and a car to get about in; Garry starting a new kind of job, and Jo with two little ones and the other coming. It was a strenuous time, for all of us, grandparents included.

At Christmas and Easter they filled our small house so that I felt the walls had to be made of elastic, stretching to fit in not so much everyone as everything – clothes, blankets, pillows, toys, games, books – and nappies! An incredible amount of impedimenta seemed to come with them. The incommodious kitchen was fit to burst with extra food and drink and Barbara in the middle of it, and little feet pattering on the way out or in the back door. Easter was more crowded than Christmas because cold, and everything happened round the fire in the one small dining/lounge room. Bare bodies drying off after baths – little garments warming on the fireguard – adults sitting either side drinking coffee or beer – games of Ludo or Snakes and Ladders on the hearth rug – by special favour the dobbing in of pine cones for kids to watch the quick catch and pretty burn. The putting to bed, the reading of stories, the kissings goodnight. It was rich and lovely, but it wasn't always easy.

It's over now – such a short time, gone so quickly – but even yet I wonder how I did it (and Whit too). It wasn't always easy, true, true. There may be cases where the elder parents are in benign accord with how the grandchildren are being handled, but I've never heard of one. My generation believed that kids should be *brought up*, taught and trained, given rules on how to behave and how to tackle life (as we were ourselves, heaven knows). The lot below us have swung to the ultimate opposite, and their faith is that kids should be left alone to make up their own minds from the very beginning, and so they'll learn for themselves how to be responsible people. It all makes for confusion in a grannie's house, heart and mind, and I confess I used to do a bit of fretting until one day, through something I was reading, I was struck with a dazzling light: the way Jo and Garry bring up their kids is *none of my business*. The way I handle them myself is my business, sure enough, but that's all. I'd thought I knew this, of course, but knowing with my brain was one thing, and with my whole guts another thing entirely. Glorious, glorious freedom!

We used to have fun when the children were old enough to come and stay 'without Daddy and Mummy'; there was more space, for one thing (physical and emotional) and I could give myself over to them. Both the girls were clever at music, lucky little things, and loved to sing together, making up harmonies. 'Scarborough Fair' for example, what a delight! The family moved to Ballarat six years ago, and when we went to collect the children and bring them back for school holidays the girls would sing us all the way home. And as for kids' concerts! One of the joys of life. It's sad those days have gone. As well as sing, the imaginative plays they'd create! And the ingenious dressing up! One of my brainwaves, stumped for gift ideas one Christmas, was getting a bundle of 'pre-loved' nighties, petticoats, frilly things, from the Op Shop. It was a wonder to see what they did with them.

The drawing and painting was a joy, especially at first. The early pictures they both did were rippers, full of bold colour and movement. Anna's 'Singapore Airport at Night', done in chalk, and months after the flight home, is a stunner and is still stored in my treasure box. But with the pencils on paper, Lucy did what Anna did. At first she was drawing nurses by the umpteen dozen, in a vivid memory of having her tonsils out in England; and all the same, with a cross on their caps and a watch on their bosoms. So Lucy drew nurses, but imagine my delight when I'd see the watch upside down, or watches all over them, legs, arms and all. When Anna was doing neat and tidy landscapes with folding hills and tiny farms with houses, fences, cows and pigs Lucy did these too. They'd go looking round the garden for bits of soft stone in colours of brown, fawn, grey, yellow, and grind these to powder, then mix them with water to make the paint for these pictures. I've tried to preserve some of them with hairspray, but I fear their life will be short. Next, the scrap paper I always provided in plenty was covered with ladies, always the same and very boring. I wondered, sadly, where the lovely bright fire of five and six years old had gone. Then it was horses, Anna's specialty. She drew horses, horses, horses for years, becoming adept with soft pencil and doing charming work – worth framing for my study wall.

Then we came to dressing dolls, the little ones I used to buy at Coles for a dollar. Another of my brainwaves was a visit to a local factory that makes women's nighties, dressing gowns and such, and buying a big bundle of 'scrap ends', soft, silky and lovely colours, and these were handed over to 'do what you like with'. They'd sew by the hour making wonderful creations for these little dolls and, forgotten by the girls, four of them decorate my study yet. Here is the place for a couple of pieces I wrote about those times:

GRANNIE ON TOAST

There's this dainty little doll standing on the mantelpiece; six inches high with shining nylon hair and a pretty face, and Oh! so charmingly dressed in a perfectly elegant gown of floral cotton with lace at the wrists and a sash to match, and a saucy tip-tilted hat. Exquisitely done; anyone would say so, not only the doting Gran of the 13-year-old *modiste*. It stands there, a cheerful reminder of the recurring *motif*, the beseeching voices of those ten days. 'Gran have you got … (a stapler, an old tennis ball, some sticky tape, any scrap paper?). 'Gran, could you find any scraps of material, any bits of old lace or ribbon? And some scissors, and we really need two pairs?' … What of that floral cotton gown? Brand-new material that just happened to be around in the shape of a pillow case, perfectly good, now utterly cut into and done for. 'Oh well,' says the Dotard to herself, 'what's a pillow case?'

This is in the first few days of the ten. The tenderly appealing *motif* seems to get more frequent, more demanding, more strident with each succeeding one. Comes the morning of the fourth.

Dotard has just pegged out two sheets and a pair of seven-year-old's pyjamas, casualty of an accident the night before (in their user's words, 'When I have a good clear sleep I'm all right. It's when I have a rough bumpy one that I wet the bed'). She has also pegged out fourteen dozen pairs of teeny weeny widgy knickers and pants, and half a hundred pairs of variform socks. She thinks of a nice cup of coffee, goes to the fridge for some milk, sees a plateful of minced steak which is crying out 'Lunch, woman!' Pronto she gets her hands into a mess of steak, onions, breadcrumbs and tomato sauce. And there sounds that *motif*: 'Gran, have you got any old plates or saucepans we could have for our cubbies? We really want three of everything because we each have our own cubby.' With her hands full of hamburger doings Dotard could find it in herself to say 'Curse your coloured cubbies!' But she doesn't, does she? She goes hunting in cupboards, doesn't she? D.D.D. – Damn, Dopey, Dotard.

Comes the evening of the seventh day. She feels she has successfully worn the day down. Shopping has been done (worst beseech of all, 'Can we come too?' 'Oh well, all *right*.') Kitchen cupboards have been attended to and supplies replenished (including an enormous packet of cereal – how can anybody at all, even a seven-year-old boy, eat eight Weet Bix for breakfast?). The bottle of boiled lollies kept for rewards and silencers has been refilled. The Gardens have been revisited and played in. Three meals for five people have been accomplished. Bodies have been bathed, teeth cleaned, the last game of Checkers played, and the darlings, suitably read-to or reading, are all in bed. The boy went first, and Dotard heard him talking there on his own and asked

'What's this about?' 'I was just talking to my penis,' he says, 'and promising him two boiled lollies if he doesn't wet the bed tonight.'

At last Dotard settles comfy, cosy (albeit creaky) by the TV to relax. But that nagging *motif* appears again, in an eleven-year-old female voice, 'Gran, have you got a spare toothbrush, a little one? I haven't cleaned my dolly's teeth.' If memory serves me rightly Dotard says in a well-controlled voice that it wouldn't hurt for once if she used her own.

Comes the day before going home. The pattern is as before, the emphasis now on getting all floppy jumpers and tight jeans clean and ironed, the spare room being tidied and all the bits bits bits (cloth, paper, felt pens, paint brushes, books, dress-ups) put or thrown away ... the *motif* surely silences *pro tem*? Not it. In a gentle, seven-year-old male voice it says 'Gran, have you got a balloon?' Dotard is defeated at last, and says, No, she just hasn't – what would he want one for? Well, he was thinking, says he, about wetting his bed. If we had a balloon and a piece of string we could fix it so the sheets wouldn't get wet. But we'd have to tie it very tight he supposed.

You are a dear little boy, my grandson, and I love you very much, but I'm glad I didn't have a balloon.

FRANK AND THE KIDS

It was one day in the last week of the school holidays. My friend Frank rang to say he had a tree full of delicious plums and perhaps the children would like some to eat? Poor lonely Frank. His wife died six years ago, and he still insists, with passion, on living by himself in the big house. 'It's home for the family, you see,' he tells us, 'whenever they can come up I want them to feel it's always here for them – home. See that? Even if it's only once a year.' His family is grown up and all four of them very busy getting on with their city lives, which don't have much time in them for trips to our country town.

Those he imagined feasting on his plums were our three grandchildren, parked with us for part of the holidays – a mutual benefit deal. I told Frank I'd be up with the kids and a bucket later on in the day. And, I added, would it be OK if Anna had a play on his piano?

'Of course, of course,' he said, 'though the poor old thing must need tuning pretty badly. I mightn't be home, but it doesn't matter. The house is always open, always. Never lock it. The plum tree is up the back, beautiful damsons, just getting ripe. The birds are starting to go for them, so do come and get some.'

Pushing through the gate and walking up the path to the front steps and the open door, I thought how seldom I go there nowadays, and how often and often I used to. Frank's wife Joan was a marvellous friend of mine over fifteen years, and we shared a big slice of our lives. But since her death Frank tells me, 'No, don't come up. I'll come to see you. The place is a bit of a mess. The front garden is about all I can manage.'

His heart, like his house, is always open, but there are spaces of the spirit where Frank has his true dwelling, and no-one visits him there.

'Look at the roses!' cried the girls, as we went past a bed of his best-beloved flowers. 'Isn't this one a gorgeous pink! And this red one! Smell it Gran!'

But I could only see the elegant stone pots on either side of the steps, that Joan had paid a packet for, wanting riotous cascades of brilliant pelargoniums to tumble there, now forlornly empty.

'Anyone home?'

No answer. We walked in, still calling as we went along the wide hall, and then out of the back door.

'Ah, Frank must be out. What a pity!' sighed Anna, fifteen and at the romantic age.

'Where's this plum tree?' called Corley, ten and ready for action.

'What a lovely big garden!' cried Lucy, thirteen, big eyes wide to beauty.

As for me, I saw the wild tangle of banksia rose climbing recklessly over the back fence; the bed and trellis, now abandoned, where Joan used to grow her delicious beans; the tall golden grasses bristling through the rough heap of wood left over from last winter.

And when we found the plum tree – havoc! Thick with little purple fruit, all, all rifled by the birds, semi-carcasses, not quite stripped and still hanging.

'What a pity – Oo – all those lovely plums …'

'Get right in the middle, there's still some good ones …'

'Watch where you're treading in your sandals, Corley …'

'Oh dear me, I can't even make jam with this lot …'

We left the poor plums to the birds, and went foraging further.

'A beautiful apple tree! Too green to eat though, worse luck.'

'Look at these enormous old pear trees! Simply covered. Frank'll have hundreds.'

'Tell him I'll come by when they're ripe and climb up and get them for him.'

I know these pears. Buckets and buckets of them brought to me every autumn, somewhat flawed with codlin.

'Oh!' cries Lucy, 'I just love this garden. I wish I could pick it all up and put it down in Ballarat for us to live in.'

Young musician Anna, bereft for two weeks, wants to look for Frank's piano. We wipe Corley's purple feet on the long grass and go into the house, and find it in the corner of the old sitting room.

'Did Joan ever play?'

'No, not ever, they were too poor when she was young for pianos. But the girls all learned when they were kids, Merle especially. She was like you Anna, mad on music.'

The lass tries it out, decided it's not too bad considering, and starts playing – gone away into her own world. Corley gets into the recliner chair given to Frank when he retired and fiddles happily with its mechanism. Lucy goes to the fireplace and the elaborate overmantel with its many little decorative partitions.

'Look at all these gorgeous photos!' and she takes them down lovingly, one by one. Joan with brilliant smile, in cap and gown; Joan with one baby, Joan with two children, three, four; Joan and Frank in family groups. 'This must be their wedding photo – wasn't she pretty! And the lovely dress – look Anna, at the beautiful train!'

'Poor Frank,' says Anna, 'It's so sad, all on his own. Oh Gran, I do hope you keep going till I'm an adult!'

'Why's that darling?'

'Oh, I just want you to be around then.'

'How old do you reckon you'll need to be for an adult? Twenty-five?'

'Yes, I suppose about then.'

'Well I might manage to keep alive for ten more years ...'

'What about me? *Twelve* more,' says Lucy.

'And me?' comes in Corley. 'How old are you now, Gran?'

'Seventy-two'.

'And I'm only nine. So you'll have to live for sixteen years, and you'll be eighty-eight. Do you think you can?'

'Better try, hadn't I? And what about Whit?'

'Oh,' says Anna, with a giggle, 'you'll have to die at the same time, you two – get whizzed up to heaven together in a wurley-wurley.'

That settled, she goes back to the piano, and I sit and take in the room. Two mattresses heaped up on top of the couch, an unlikely wardrobe by the wall and next to it a heap of cardboard cartons, the sideboard with its transparent door showing still Joan's treasures of china and glassware, and on the top her beautiful blue vase with three withering gladioli in it; the whole room cluttered with odd pieces of furniture. But what I really see, and so vividly, is the coffee table covered with bowls of nuts, cheese, biscuits and cabana, the top of the side table bearing frosty bottles of beer and flagons of wine. Good talk, gaiety, friendship, warmth – can a person feel the ghost of an atmosphere?

But Anna brings me back, blithely, to the here and now. She is playing a romping piece of her own composing, filling the room with the essence of youthfulness and fun.

And I become aware of Frank standing in the doorway, listening – and Oh! the smile in his eyes, the light in his face!

NEW ELEMENTS ~ THE OLD

In spite of creaky knees and cranky back, I never think of myself as growing old; I realise I must be when our Anna turns eighteen, when a niece achieves her fourth grandchild, when I go to visit Frank who lives now, precariously, in a Home and Hospital for the Aged. Then I think about it and when I see in my life about me old people, living on their own in houses, fragile, failing and falling about, I wonder what I will be like if this comes to me. Will I cling ever and ever more desperately to my home with my 'things' about me, to the familiar pattern of my days; and be prostrated with dread at the prospect of upheaval and going into the unknown? Will I keep saying I'm not ready yet to go to 'one of those places,' not yet, not *yet*, and so becoming more and more of a bind and a burden, probably to my dearly-loved daughter?

I like to think I could be like my sister Nan. She looked herself fair in the eye when she was coming up towards eighty, on her own and with her body on its downhill slope, and she prepared herself for her likely future. Still in passable health and able to look after herself, she sold her dear little house and went to live in a Retirement Village. She had a self-contained unit with its own kitchen and bathroom, sitting and bedroom, and space for a bit of garden. I had to brace myself when I first went to see her there, to accept Nan living in so small a space, my Nan, a boundless person if ever there was one. She was a student of Art to begin with, then Headmistress of her own school, but a student of life always, ever ready to learn, and with an inexhaustible love of people, especially young ones.

I got used to it. She was happy enough there for a few years, independent within the community, still driving her own car and caring for herself entirely, getting great pleasure from growing irises and lacanalias, and enjoyment as Great-aunt when young relations came to visit. Some times she entertained with little lunches and dinners. Then the time came when her body told her she couldn't do all this for much longer, and she planned to go to another Village, one where she'd be totally cared for, in any eventuality – and where she'd be living in one room, a room so small she called it her 'sardine tin'.

LETTER TO NAN

You and I, with Ian and his wife Betty – how well we can all remember the time we got you ready for making this move. You had various battles with your body; a stomach ulcer, problems with hearing aids, operations on your feet and toes, and now, at eighty-two, there was a big job coming up – a hip replacement. It was just bad luck that your surgeon had an unexpected vacancy for this about a month before you were due to move. You had to make the decision – grab the chance, when it mightn't come again for months? Or wait and get yourself all sorted out and organised for the move? I think it was pain that decided you, along with Ian and Betty's invitation to go to them for your convalescence, and their offer to help you with the move. And you had my promise, from months back, that I'd be there to help too – couldn't let you do such a monstrous thing without your kid sister, could I?

So off for the operation you, and some weeks later, off to Sydney me. I was to stay with Ian and Betty as well, in their beautiful house high on the hillside at Elanora Heights, with its wonderful view right out over the ocean. The spare room was all got ready for you, and for me a corner of the big lounge/dining room was rigged up with a bed and make-shift dressing table. All that luxurious space I had! Carpet on the floor, paintings on the walls, silver on the sideboard. I told them I felt like Mae West or Lady Di.

We collected you from the hospital the day after I arrived – remember the job we had manipulating that unbendable leg into the first seat of Betty's little car? And then the two processes began; getting back your mobility, and getting the contents of your unit reduced so you could be squeezed into your pygmy dwelling.

You went to work on yourself with something like passion. So clearly I can see you, in your royal blue dressing gown and solid walking shoes, doing your regulation fifty steps every morning round the back patio, and then with your mouth set firm and determination in your eye, stomping up the flight of steps in front of the house, foot after foot. And at the top, doing your deep breathing, looking away out to sea. (You told me later you were facing the reality of your being now an old woman).

Then you'd dress, only needing help with the stockings and shoes, and after breakfast we'd settle you in the study where Betty had set up a divan close to the wide windows, and a table alongside for radio, books, writing things and such. Very cosy and comfy you were. Betty and I would leave you there and drive off to St. David's to get on with what we regarded as our part of the job (Ian being away at work).

After a few days we'd take you with your bed-chair, all the big cardboard boxes we could lay hands on, and a sandwich for our lunch. You'd sit up on the bed and give directions to our enquiries – 'What about this, Nan?' – 'Where's this to go?' That such a small unit could hold so many things! The only one of the family never married, you had a residue of furniture and pieces from our old home long ago, even to an *Encyclopedia Brittanica* in its ancient wooden revolving case. You had linen, china, crockery, vases, mirrors, household stuff – what of that wonderful antique silver fish-serving set in its velvet lined box? Paintings by the dozen, accumulated treasure of years, many of your own. Picture frames and painting gear (you had been an artist first and teacher after). Books, books, books. Letters and diaries saved for years. Lots of lovely clothes. Multifarious etceteras (including three discarded sets of top dentures). And you had to get yourself down to the bare basics for living; there'd be just room over for a radio, TV, stereogram and one shelf of books.

What a sorting out to do, what a cleaning out and up, what a giving and throwing away! By a lucky stroke of fate the Warden of St. David's was organising a jumble sale in a few weeks' time – what she copped! The big old iron chest in the storage room, where you kept precious dress-ups from old school concerts, and drawings made for you by a multitude of great-nieces and nephews for birthdays – that copped plenty too.

Oh you were brave, Nan! Out, out, out. 'What about this little bowl?' 'Oh dear, Andrew made that for me years and years ago. It's no use is it? It'll have to go.' The emotional pull, drag and pain of doing for yourself what it usually falls on someone else to do for us after we depart this life! No wonder you'd be exhausted by mid-afternoon.

Betty and I would be feeling a bit that way ourselves, so we'd take you (and the bed-chair) back to Elanora Heights, where we'd have a rest, you with a cup of tea, Betty and I with a nice cold beer, and then Betty would get food cooking. And in good time I'd help you with the shower.

What a memory, Nan! Into the bathroom (with heater on – it was June) where you'd strip and stand at the basin to soap yourself all over, and then I'd help you under the shower to wash it all off, then dry and powder you. I clearly recall you standing there in the bathroom watching over your operations, seeing your brave and ageing body, and having a feeling of love that went down, down, down through me like a pebble in a bottomless pool. Back to your room into a nightie, dressing gown and slippers, then we'd brush and do your silver hair, and so be ready for Bet's good dinner.

After that and perhaps a game of Scrabble I was on the job again to get you warm and comfy for bed. Massage the tender feet was part of it, and remember when I had the brainwave to rub your 'good' leg, which was feeling the strain, with Dencorub? I can still see my lean brown hands, with their bumpy veins and dark age-spots, going rub, rub, rub over your pale swollen leg.

It helped too, and, along with your faithful obeying of your doctor's instructions, you got stronger day by day. Every little win was a big one. The jubilation when you could put your shoes on for yourself, and soon even the pantyhose! The joy when you could sit on a stool and do Betty's ironing! (you had been so distressed at your dependence on us both).

So the two processes moved along side by side. It took three solid weeks' work at St. David's before everything was cleared, disposed of, or packed up, and at last there came the day when the removalists arrived and took all away. Betty and I were there to supervise; no need for you that day. I was glad you spared yourself the sight of the bare rooms, the empty shell of your living over six years, and really since long before that. We locked the door, gave the key to the Warden, and Betty shouted me a splendid fish lunch at Manly to celebrate what we felt was something of an achievement.

You were still only just mobile, in spite of your grand progress, and the new wing at Lady Gowrie, where you were to go, wasn't quite ready. But it was time for me to go home. So I couldn't stick to the promise I'd made to myself, to be there beside you as you walked in the new door. So it was a big hug and a kiss Goodbye, and I can see now the look in your eyes, full of love and longing, tugging at me – you didn't want me to go, did you? You wanted me to be around, near, somewhere, not only till you moved but thereafter.

And I? With all the love in me, and thanks to whatever gods gave me such a sister; with all my eleven-years-younger energy to help bathe and dress, to massage, to fill hot water bottles and bring cups of tea, and to be in attendance, with all my permeating sorrow that you had to go and live in a 'sardine tin', with all this, I could only be glad and grateful that it existed, be thankful that care, comfort and attention were there for you. And, as you told me then and I saw for myself later, everything else about the Village was spacious, and beautiful too. There were lovely grounds and garden, with a wide view and a swimming pool, a dining hall, community places, a music room and a craft room (which soon became your special territory).

You're still there, Nan, four years on, four years and a few more physical miseries, and doing a darned good job of living along, I'd say. Your life is a full and busy project, and the tiny living space where your body is hadn't curbed the size of <u>you</u> not one miniscule jot.

BIRTHDAY PARTY

Three of my sisters have turned eighty (one died when she was sixty-four). Three times I've tripped to Sydney to join the party and the family reunion. The last time was in January this year.

Our Winsome. All my sisters had each their own kind of beauty, but Winsome! Very tall, slim and fair; reserved, not spectacular at first sight in a crowded room, but after a while a stranger would have said 'Whoever's that beautiful woman!' She moved in airs of grace, glamour and elegance that endowed her with a remoteness from the mundane world, or so it always seemed to me, the Kid Sister. It lifted me out of the ordinary that she was part of our family, belonged to us.

So many gifts! Champion at sports all through High School, especially swimming and diving. Top of her year all along, and out into university with a brilliant pass. She elected to do a course rarely heard of for a woman in 1922 – Architecture. I don't know by what chance she left us and went into residence at the Women's College – how our dad could ever have let her, even with a scholarship! Perhaps because of? It would have been utterly against his grain to let one go by. Anyhow she did. And that put her into a different world from the rough and tumble of the rest of us at home, well and truly. It was a wonderful weekend when she wafted home now and then like a duchess, always looking a million on the tiny allowance Dad gave her. She had a flair for clothes, and enjoyed whipping up clever dresses for herself or picking them out of bargain racks.

When she was through she landed a job, even in Depression times when architects were peddling hairpins and stockings around town. Kept it too. Living at home again, she pinched and scraped and wore her undies until they were rags, saving, saving for the Big Trip Abroad. Which took a few years, then off she sailed for London, with just enough meagre money to live on for a month or two, and a mighty pocketful of dreams. These pretty well came true. She soon got work with a firm of architects, stayed there three years, and in her holidays had her heart's desire visiting famous cities and buildings on the Continent.

Somehow through all this, and through the year or so when she wore a golden-sapphire engagement ring, she dodged marrying and came home again when she was thirty-two, in clouds of splendor, now the brilliant career woman. She wore stunning clothes, had a Parisian hair style, smoked cigarettes in long holders and even in front of Mother, she drank – a sophisticated concoction of gin and sherry I remember – she got a job at an unbelievable salary, and she bought a car. Fantastic female!

But her luck didn't go all the way. She'd been sick in London, and she used to get agonising migraines, mostly at crisis points in her own or the family life. She'd be bowled over, flat, useless. I was the family massager, and I couldn't say how often or for how long I would stand by her bed with cold water, *eau de cologne* and a man's hanky softly, gently with my finger tips calming and soothing the poor head.

Finally her luck ran out, though not till after many years. Thirty or so, during which she married a fellow architect, produced one child, and had a life full of rewarding work, interesting activity, travel, people. Then it came, twelve years ago now. The brain tumor. The surgery. The intensive care ward. The battle for life – half-life as it turned out, her close-time memory gone, and all her incentive for living. She can remember what happened before the operation, but not yesterday or five minutes ago. She likes lying in bed – 'What is there to get up for?' she says. And she simply loves cake. It's as if she's gone back to a little girl who never had her fill of sweet things. Fat has taken her body over.

Not utter ebb tide, the luck. Eric, her husband, was always there, caring for her with a devotion and patience almost beyond belief. And when he could do it on his own no longer their daughter, Chalice – now with a husband, a son and a daughter – took them both into her home, in a downstairs flat converted from a huge billiard room.

This is where the party was held. A splendid cold buffet luncheon hosted by husband and daughter. Tables and chairs had been arranged for about thirty people, decorations had been put up by the children, flowers and fruit were on the tables, everything very festive. Bar Chalice, the only people present under the age of sixty-five were under sixteen – the children, Andrew and Moninya, with a friend apiece.

We were all there, the seven of us left in the family, with wives and husbands (except mine, who hates Sydney and won't go there), and Isobel and Norma, too, wives of the two brothers who are dead (Graham, who was married to Mary, remarried and lives in New Zealand). All of us together – the first time for many years. We generate an excitement when we get together, especially when the far-flung ones come. And Oh! How old we all looked! No matter how smartly and expensively turned out and coiffured. How old we all are!

I'd gone early, to dress Winsome and do her hair, thick stuff still and bushy now, streaky grey. Lesley had given me a rose for her to wear, an exquisite delicate creamy-pink one, and all the time I was massaging, brushing and braiding Winsome had it in her hand saying 'This is the most beautiful rose I've ever seen.' She asked me about my daughter and her family, and then five minutes later asked the same questions. She was perfectly happy – I think she'd forgotten there was a party on. I pinned the rose on her frock and, proud of my job, looked around for a mirror to let her see the effect. There wasn't one to be seen, not anywhere in the room. Eric came in, impatient because guests were arriving, and between us we got her into the big room and to her place of honour. She sat there smiling happily, surrounded by flowers, fruit, cards, gifts, looking no older than the siblings and the few close friends who flowed about her; just more composed and still.

Old, old, all of us. Coping with the insults and injuries of age with all the dignity and humour we could muster, and not doing a bad job either. I could reckon an over-all toll of major and minor operations in the last – Oh, twenty years – on toes, stomachs, hips, arthritic feet and elbows; and three heart attacks have been and gone. But apart from the common aids for teeth, sight and hearing the outward signs were no worse than one walking stick and one wheelchair. Lucky for us good, rich hair was always a thing in our family, bestowed by both our Dad and Mum, so there was a showing of beautiful white or silver heads, and not one bald one.

So. The party. Eating, drinking, talking, laughing, remembering old times. Eric made a little speech. Champagne went round. The four young fry, so charming, waited on us, girls with food and boys with drinks, and it was a cheerful party almost like any other. Someone had an instant camera, and was taking snaps of little groups about the room. When Winsome was shown one with her in it, she just said simply 'Is that me?' Most likely, we thought, she hadn't seen herself in years.

So the party wound down. Some people said Goodbye, others got together in the kitchen and belted into the washing up. Some stayed quietly yarning. The children, let free from their jobs and their good manners were suddenly a bunch of kids having fun in the pool – good swimmers all. And Winsome showed signs of weariness and wanting to retire. Eric helped her to her room and I went with them to put her to bed.

It was my undoing. The poor heavy ungainly body that can't move without help or holding on. The gentle, sweet, childlike woman; as I unpinned the drooping rose, still telling me it was the most beautiful she'd ever seen, and saying it had been a lovely party but she'd just like to get to bed now.

'Oh darling, wait till I get your dress off and your nightie on.'

With a little laugh, 'I thought I was in my nightie.'

'What! Your pretty new dress! Come on, let me help you off with it.'

Not so easily done either. A matter of getting long skirts pulled up around waist, sitting her on the side of the bed while I got them over her head, and then reverse performance with the nightie. Eric was there to help me hold her and lift the thick legs.

At last I had her snug in bed, the dress hung up, the hair unpinned and in two plaits, the rose in water on the dressing table, and she sighed with content. I tucked her up and gently kissed her goodbye.

I managed to get through the party room and out into the garden before my tears disgraced me. Strange how a person can stand absolutely still, not moving at all, and tears just falling down the face. The only one to see me was Bob, who got me together with a hanky and a cigarette, and then – then I was saved. Saved indeed. Young, bright, merry, a voice at my side:

'Come for a swim, Auntie Barbara?'

Moninya. Aged eleven. Beautiful brown wet body in a blue swim suit, blue eyes laughing, black hair sleek down her back. With her Joanna, same age, just as brown and beautiful, with a red swimsuit and the sleek hair blonde.

'I'd love to. No bathers though.'

'You can borrow Mum's.'

'Never fit me.'

'She's got an old one that's stretched – come on, please, *please*.'

What an abiding richness they gave me! At night time when I can't sleep, one of my lurks is to go over with my mind's eye some lovely happening that I remember. This is one of my best. Those two glorious kids, swimming, diving, jumping, somersaulting, showing off a treat for me – and perhaps for the boys, now loafing on the balcony? – doing all their tricks. 'Just watch and we'll do the routine we made up.' Brimming with fun and vitality, they swam, dived, leapt the length of the pool, in their element like a couple of shining young dolphins, one blue, one red.

11. L'Envoi

This brings my story up to now, and I can't go any farther. I've done what I set out to do, and tried to sort out some of the unresolved things stored in the cupboard of my mind. I've said some 'Thank-yous' for the goodness that came my way, but I don't know that I've expressed enough 'I'm sorrys' for the mistakes I've made and the hurt that I've dished out. I'll say one big one now to cover them all, and hope that by now I've paid back at least as much as I owe, if not in the same directions. But one big, great big Thank-you remains.

LETTER TO DARBY FROM JOAN

There's a place called Angourie, and it's one of the most beautiful places we know. It's still unspoiled, undeveloped, un-upbuggered; wonderful to say, still as nature made it. There's a grassy hump shoving itself out into the sea between two beaches, with heaped smooth grey rocks and wind-bent casuarina trees leaning over, their fine fronds swaying. There's a steep sandy track pitching down from the cliff-top to the northern beach, between a tangle of lantana and banksia bushes. There's a more kindly track ambling down to the southern one, and this is the one for us. There's lantana too, and the old banksias, twisted and knobbly, but most of it tufty scrub, starred, if you look, with tiny wild flowers, gold, blue, pink, purple. Everywhere among the sharp grass there's low-growing spiky wattle, and all about us the voices of the little singing birds that love this place, and the constant crashy sound of the sea.

We go there often when we're away on our winter holiday. One morning, though the sun is blazing away, there's a great wind blowing from the south and a tremendous sea is running. You hurry me up. 'The sooner we can get there the better,' you say, 'the boys are sure to be out.' And they are. From the top of the steep side we can see twenty or more of them out there in the surf where the swell humps up round the point, like strange sea creatures, lying on their boards waiting for the breakers just as they start to curl. This is Angourie, famous on the coast for the roll and shape of its waves; this is the beach for the experts, the champions, the wizards of the surfing world. With a sea like today's a fellow has to be a maestro even to get himself on his board way out beyond the turmoil of waters to catch his ride.

We make off for the beach down our favourite track, laden for the day. We are in old slacks, shirts and jumpers, you have a hat and I a scarf round my blowing hair. You are carrying a picnic basket, two sand-chairs, and a mini-esky. Rowley is out in front sniffing and running in dog-ecstasy. I come along behind with a bag that holds bathing togs and towels, and truth to tell, in case I weary of watching blokes surfing, my book and glasses. Once we used to feel ourselves a pair of old fuddy-duddies carrying all this tackle, but we got over that – comfort is all, and who cares?

At the bottom of the hillside we get among bumpy sand dunes between the two beaches. Tucked out of the wind are some girls sun-baking; breasts, legs and thighs all bare and brown. They're so pretty! They only wear a G-string with a miniscule triangle of cloth back and front. Your admiration is pure and simple, but mine is mingled with envy – how lovely to get into the sun and the sea clad in just so much and no more! Once I would have – I can remember being very dashing thirty odd years ago in one of the first two-piecers seen on Bondi – but not now. It's aesthetics, not modesty that makes me sigh. The turn-out I wear now is as good as neck-to-knee by comparison. It even has a small skirt that drapes itself discreetly over bumps and bulges.

We go on past the dunes to our pet spot under the shelter of the humpy bit. You dig away at the sand and wedge my chair into a firm support for my back, and plonk your own down. We get into our cossies and settle ourselves. The sun belts down on us. And there, in front of our eyes, is the greatest free show on earth, on land or sea. We go into raptures watching the riding of the waves. The beauty of it, the skill, the artistry, the magic, the wonder! How can they! 'Look at that!' you cry as some chap catches a huge wave, shoots it down as it breaks, turns and goes skimming along the tunnel, twists as the break catches up with him, shoots it again and comes speeding towards shore, turning at last and gliding off the wave so as to miss the rocky edges. Then paddling back for another go. True, sometimes, helter-skelter, someone disappears into a dumper; but like a miracle, appears again. Gradually we pick out our favourites. 'There's the boy in red! What a champion! Here comes the one with the striped suit – isn't he superb! Bravo boy, bravo!' you cry.

The wind's too cold for our usual surf on the other beach, so we stay put till lunch time. While we are eating our salad sandwiches we think of the magnificent hunger those boys have when they come out; we imagine their teeth chomping into a good hunk of steak, with some chips and maybe a few sausages to fill up the gaps. You almost relish the hunger in your own vitals, your spirit has been riding waves all morning.

After lunch, back into our clothes and a walk across the narrow span of sand to the tumble of rocks on the far side. Someone sitting in the shelter of the dunes gives us a smile and a nod of the head, and we recognise the young chap we gave a lift to the other day, going back to Yamba. He told us he'd hurt his back surfing and was on his way to see a doctor. He was living in the bush near Angourie, he said – giving it a go, might make his dole spin out better that way. We'd seen him sitting there a few times since, always on his own, always looking the same, just sitting, watching, next to him his board and a plastic bag with a few green apples in it. The sad sack, we called him.

His speech was thick and hard to understand, his face dull and expressionless. The long tangled hair, bleached yellow on top and showing ginger underneath, made my fingers itch for a tub of good hot water and a big bar of soap. He wore long trousers, the old-fashioned kind, stretchy with tapered legs, and below them we could see the hems of his long johns, which also hadn't been near soap and water in a long, long time. On top he had an old brown jumper, the wool unravelling round big holes in the elbows. Does he go into the water in this gear, we wonder? Couldn't afford the usual wet-suit, of course. Has he anyone in the world who cares about him? We say Hullo and he tells us his back is much better, and we wish him luck.

Now we reach the rocks that will take us round to a wide ledge, clean cut down to the water, specially designed you'd think for a good big roller to come smacking onto, with an almighty Crump! And a shooting of spray high into the air – with us shouting for the glory of it. But getting there isn't all so easy today, the rocks are wet and slippery and we wish our legs were more reliable rock-hoppers.

I've called your legs 'Willy and Wally' because the left one has been misbehaving and might give a sharp twinge and then crumple just when it shouldn't. You look regretfully at a sizey gap between two rocks and say 'Bugger you Willy! Once a chap would have jumped that and thought nothing of it.' You find a way round. I look at it with similar regret, and as the dog springs lightly over, I say 'I wish I had four lively little legs like you have, Rowley.' I decide there's only one way for me and that's use my bottom, so I sit and stretch across limb by limb.

So we go, and make the ledge, and have our reward in a wonderful wave-watch. Here we come abreast with another couple of our vintage. They have come from the other direction, down a path. She is a blue-rinse lady, in a smart pink jump suit, he has a tweed cap and a fine hand-knitted sweater outlining his pot belly. We say to one another 'Good afternoon, bit of a breezy day, beautiful spot isn't it, lovely place,' and I move on. You seem to be caught in conversation. You call me back and introduce me, 'Barbara this is Hec Richardson, and his wife Allie.' The man is grinning and beaming and stuttering with delight.

'Whaddayerknow! From the old Battery! I said to myself when I saw you, if that's not Alf Whitley I'll go he. Alf Whitley!' and turning to his wife, 'That's the bloke, when we were in Syria, used to get out in the morning and roll naked in the snow.'

'Oh, I've heard of him,' says the wife, with a dutiful smile, 'they all thought he was crazy.'

'Nothing crazy about it,' you say. 'Perfectly sensible. There weren't any showers. A good way to get clean, and I felt great after it.'

'Whaddayerknow!' the fellow says again. 'Alf Whitley! That's two chaps we've met from the old Battery, other times we don't meet anyone. Just yesterday bumped into Reg Carney – you remember him?'

'Can't say I do,' you say, but we stand there and chat about Yamba and what a beautiful place it is. You say we've been having a fantastic time watching the boys surfing and aren't they superb, and Hec says, 'Yes , I suppose so, but I always have to wonder, how many of them are really chaps on holiday or are they just dole bludgers, ought to be out somewhere doing a good day's work.'

We let that pass. No use getting into an argument on such a day; and after Hec says they're staying in the caravan park and we might bump into each other again we move on, hearing murmurs of 'Whaddayerknow!' fading on the air.

We finish our beautiful walk to the next bay and back, we get ourselves over the tumble of rocks again, we collect our gear and make our way up the sandy track to the car (the air still full of bird songs), and so we set off for our holiday flat.

You tell me you haven't any recollection of this Hec Richardson, but think you can remember Reg Carney.

'If that's the one,' you tell me, 'he was a very good-looking chap, tall and dark, really handsome. I can remember him because he used to tell us his way with the girls. No time for mucking around, he used to say, ask them Do you do it or don't you, and if they say no just pass on to the next one.'

I suggest you don't tell that to the wife if we bump into them.

'Hell', you say, 'I hope we don't. Spare me those dreary old army reminiscences – nothing bores me more.' I fancy I suffer them worse than you do.

But it seems we are fated for it. A few days later, sure enough, you bump into Hec Richardson in the paper shop. Hec is in the same caravan park as Reg Carney (Whaddayerknow!) and when he told Reg Carney about meeting Alf Whitley, Reg said he'd really love to meet him again, he just had to; so one evening, you told him, we'd take a couple of bottles and go off to the caravan park and find them.

We put it off till our last evening, so there'd be no chance of any carry-on, and went to the pub for a couple of bottles. But the pub stands high up on the hill between river and ocean, and there was a gorgeous sunset, clouds blazing red in the west and glowing pink in the east. How could we be bothered with any Reg Carneys in caravans? We sat together in the car looking over Yamba Bay, a beer in our hands, and watched the fishing trawlers going out to sea in the quiet of the evening, till the colours all faded and the dark came down.

www.ingramcontent.com/pod-product-compliance
Lightning Source LLC
LaVergne TN
LVHW051518070426
835507LV00023B/3182